WHY? BECAUSE. BECAUSE WHY?

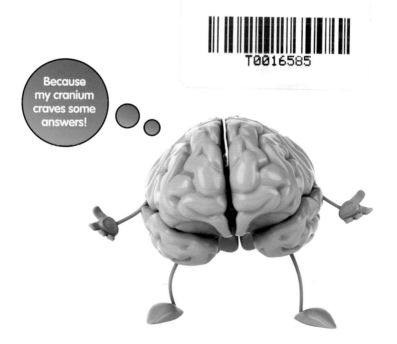

Because my cranium craves some answers!

T0016585

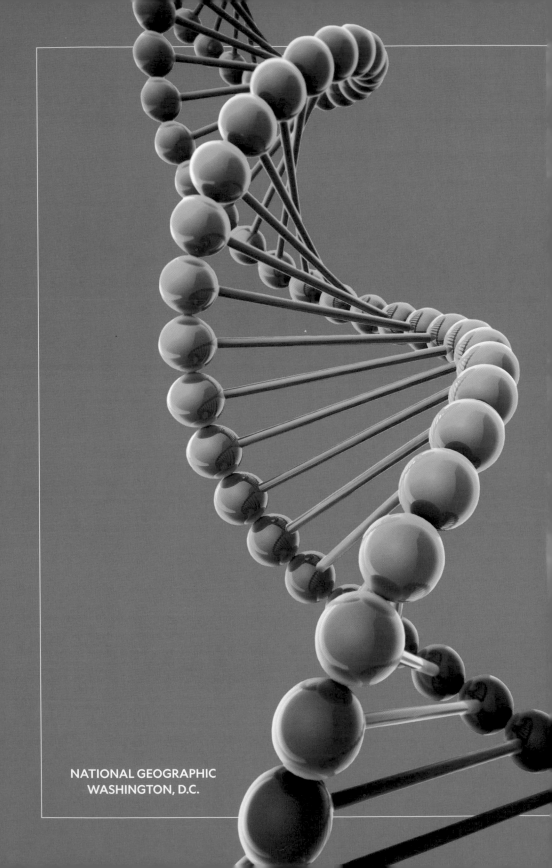

NATIONAL GEOGRAPHIC
WASHINGTON, D.C.

NATIONAL
GEOGRAPHIC
KiDS

WHY?

THE HUMAN BODY

99+ AWESOME ANSWERS FOR CURIOUS KIDS

PAIGE TOWLER

WHY
DON'T **HUMANS** HAVE **WINGS?**

WHAT
IS YOUR **BRAIN** MADE OF?

CAN
HUMANS **CLONE THEMSELVES?**

WHY
DO **PEOPLE** LOOK SO **DIFFERENT** FROM **EACH OTHER?**

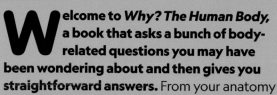

Welcome to *Why? The Human Body,* a book that asks a bunch of body-related questions you may have been wondering about and then gives you straightforward answers. From your anatomy (Why is blood red? Why do people have eyebrows?) to your senses (Why can't we see in the dark? Why do we think some scents stink?), some of the human body's greatest curiosities are explained. You'll even get answers to questions you might not have thought to ask: Why do people have snot? What would happen to your body if you lived on Mars?

And there's more. Take a quiz to see how brainy you are about brains or a quiz to get a *sense* for how well you know your sense of taste. Quick preview: Your brain is mostly made of ... (*Psst:* It's probably not what you'd think!)

You'll also hear from experts, such as a neuroscientist—a scientist who studies brains—who is learning how to enhance, remove, and change memories. (And—bonus!—he also gives advice on how to boost your memory power.)

By the end of this book, your brain will be as full of answers as it is of neurons. What exactly is a neuron and what does it do, you wonder? Turn to page 102 to find out!

CONTENTS

WHY do BONES BREAK?

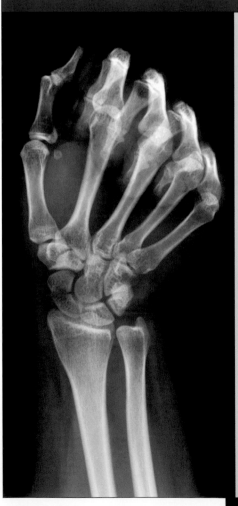

***Ouch!* Anyone who's suffered from a cracked or broken bone knows that it's no fun.** So why is it even possible for part of your skeleton to break in the first place? The answer has to do with what bones are made of and what they do. Your bones are living tissue, and they are made of a type of protein called collagen. Collagen gives bones their structure. Bones are also made of a mineral called calcium phosphate, which adds strength and sturdiness. Bones do lots of things: For example, they give you your shape, protect your internal organs, and even make cells—the tiny building blocks that make up all living organisms. So why aren't bones made from a stronger material? Because bones must be strong enough to hold you up but also light and flexible enough to help you move!

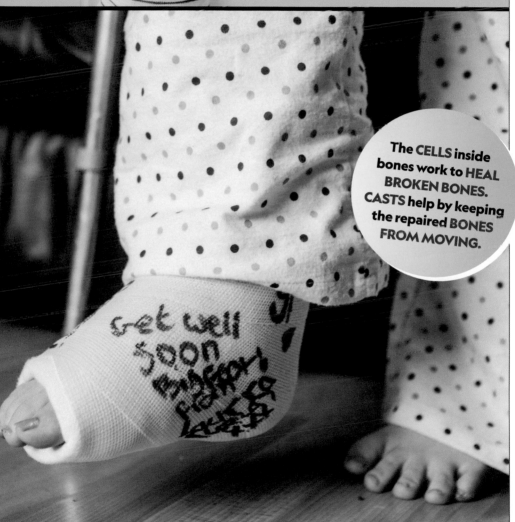

SAY WHAT?!

A NEWBORN BABY HAS ABOUT 300 BONES, COMPARED TO AN ADULT'S 206. (THIS IS BECAUSE BONES FUSE AS YOU AGE.)

The CELLS inside bones work to HEAL BROKEN BONES. CASTS help by keeping the repaired BONES FROM MOVING.

Get well soon

A HUMAN'S SPINE HAS 33 BONES, BUT A SNAKE'S CAN HAVE AS MANY AS 600!

SAY WHAT?!

WHY don't I have FUR?

Well, most people *do* have fur ... on their head! Fur is just the word that people use to describe the hair on nonhuman animals.

OK, so why don't people have hair that covers their bodies like animals do? The short answer is this: Scientists don't really know! Almost all other mammals have fur—even our fellow primates, such as gorillas and chimpanzees. Most scientists think humans are relatively smooth and hairless as a result of something called thermoregulation. This process, seen when dogs pant or humans sweat, is how many animals keep their body temperatures within a certain range. Millions of years ago, as human ancestors moved into hot, open grasslands, they might have lost body hair so that they could hunt during the day without getting overheated. And if they needed to get warm, they eventually had a new discovery for that: controlled fire!

chimpanzee

Hair Today, Gone Tomorrow

Don't worry—we're not alone. Humans aren't the only mammals that lack a thick fur coat. One hairless mammal even bears the description in its name: the naked mole rat. Known for their wrinkly, bald skin, naked mole rats spend almost all their time underground. This means that they don't need hair to protect them from the sun or keep them warm. But even so, they aren't completely hairless. Naked mole rats have long hairs between their toes to help them dig dirt, as well as long whiskers on their face to help them find their way around.

naked mole rat

Like naked mole rats, many other mammals don't need fur because of where they live. Large animals on the African savanna, such as elephants, rhinoceroses, and hippopotamuses, have very little hair so they can stay cool in their hot grassland homes. For mammals that live entirely in the water, such as dolphins, hair serves no purpose. (Dolphins are born with some hair around the snout and head, but it usually falls out as they age.) But what about those hairless dog breeds? They were bred to be that way!

Chinese crested dog

Some scientists think that our **HUMAN ANCESTORS** may have **LOST THEIR HAIR** because it helped them get rid of **BODY LICE** and other parasites.

THE BALD UAKARI MONKEY HAS A FACE THAT IS NOT ONLY BALD BUT BRIGHT RED.

WHAT does my BLOOD DO?

What doesn't your blood do?
From nonstop delivery service to waste removal to warrior-worthy defense, blood does it all. One of blood's most important functions is to carry oxygen, which humans need to survive, throughout your body. To do this, it relies on your circulatory system. The circulatory system is made up of veins and arteries. As your heart beats, it sends blood and oxygen through arteries to other parts of your body. Veins carry blood back to the heart. Your heart also sends blood to your lungs to pick up more oxygen. And there's so much more! Blood carries nutrients and important chemicals called hormones throughout your body. Hormones act as messengers that deliver information to different parts of your body, such as when to grow (see p. 18) or when to feel hungry (see p. 116). Blood also carries away waste like carbon dioxide, a gas that our body creates from the oxygen we breathe in. Blood helps fight off infections and heal wounds, too.

JELLYFISH don't have CIRCULATORY SYSTEMS ... or blood at all!

WHY is my BLOOD RED?

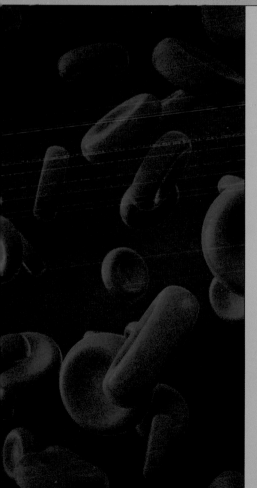

Your blood is made up of small units called blood cells and plasma. Plasma is a mix of water, proteins, fats, sugars, and salts. It carries the blood cells—plus nutrients, hormones, and waste—through your body. As for the blood cells, there are two types: white and red. White blood cells help fight off infections. Because your body only needs them at certain times, there are fewer white blood cells than red blood cells. But if your body encounters an infection, it will make more. Red blood cells help carry oxygen through your body, thanks to a protein called hemoglobin. Hemoglobin binds to the oxygen, helping it travel with your blood. Hemoglobin also appears red, which makes your blood look red!

Some animals—such as certain kinds of OCTOPUSES and SPIDERS—have BLUE BLOOD.

WHY can't I FLY?

It seems unfair—why do birds get to fly through the clouds? Why don't *we* have wings? The answer is simple: We don't need them. Humans excel at surviving on the ground. Even if we *did* have feathery flappers, we still wouldn't be able to take to the skies. Humans are very big and very heavy compared to birds (and bats). To lift all our weight, we would need *enormous* wings. And even if we did have wings that big, we wouldn't be strong enough to use them. Human muscles are designed to help us run, leap, grab, and balance—not to flap gigantic wings. The characteristics that make humans great at living on land also keep us from soaring in the sky. It seems that flying is truly for the birds.

The **RÜPPELL'S GRIFFON VULTURE** can **FLY** as **HIGH** as 36,000 FEET (11,000 m)—about the height of a **CRUISING AIRPLANE.**

Build-a-Bird

Hang on. If a human with gigantic wings would be too weak to fly, how did enormous pterosaurs take flight some 215 million years ago? The answer lies in the anatomy of these ancient flying reptiles—and their modern-day bird relatives. Unlike humans, birds and their ancient relatives have hollow bones. Birds also have special air sacs inside their bodies that make them even lighter, as well as strong chest muscles that allow them to flap their wings. Scientists think that pterosaurs had all of these, too.

SCIENTISTS THINK THAT BABY PTERODACTYLS COULD FLY ALMOST AS SOON AS THEY WERE BORN.

WHY aren't people MORE COLORFUL?

Red, blue, green, yellow … animals around the world seem to come in a rainbow of colors. Some animals can even change colors! So why don't humans have more of a variety of skin and hair tones? For humans and many other animals, the colors of their hair, skin, and eyes are caused by something called melanin. Humans have two kinds of melanin that determine color: eumelanin and pheomelanin. Eumelanin creates brown and black shades. People with a lot of eumelanin in their skin, eyes, or hair will have darker coloring in those areas. People with less eumelanin will have lighter coloring. Pheomelanin creates red and yellow shades and can lead to red hair. But why don't humans have more kinds of melanin? Scientists think that black, brown, and beige shades would have helped human ancestors blend into their surroundings to stay safe or hunt.

SAY **WHAT?!**

BLUE-FOOTED BOOBIES GET THE COLORING OF THEIR BLUE FEET FROM THE FISH THEY EAT.

MELANIN ALSO HELPS PROTECT SKIN FROM SOME OF THE SUN'S RAYS.

SAY **WHAT?!**

IN SOME ANIMALS, MORE MELANIN CAN APPEAR IN SOME PLACES THAN OTHERS, LEADING TO SPOTS AND STRIPES!

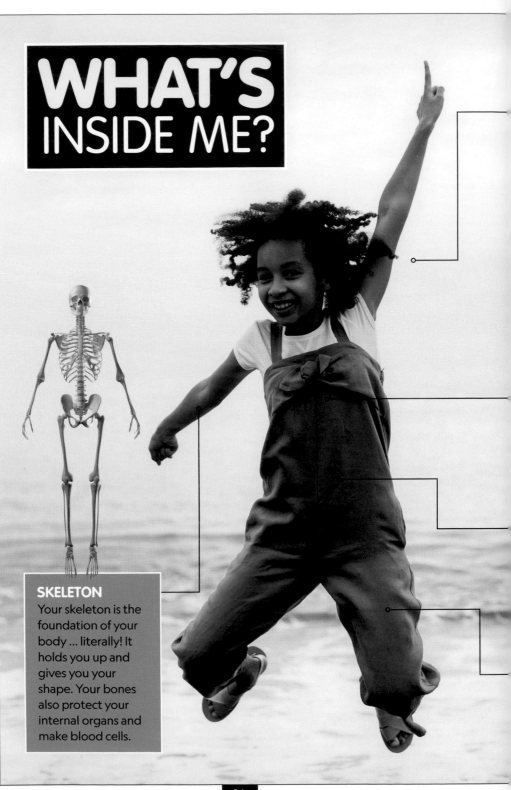

WHAT'S INSIDE ME?

SKELETON
Your skeleton is the foundation of your body ... literally! It holds you up and gives you your shape. Your bones also protect your internal organs and make blood cells.

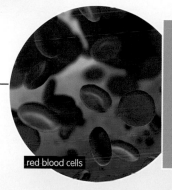
red blood cells

CIRCULATORY SYSTEM

Your circulatory system refers to your blood vessels, your arteries and veins, and the blood that flows through them. Your heart pumps blood through your body and to your lungs to pick up oxygen. Your blood carries important things such as oxygen, nutrients, and hormones. Blood also helps fight infections.

RESPIRATORY SYSTEM

Think of your respiratory system and your circulatory system as teammates. The respiratory system works with the circulatory system to help you breathe. Your airways—your mouth, nose, and throat—bring air to your lungs. Your circulatory system then brings oxygen from your lungs to the rest of your body. The respiratory system also helps get rid of waste such as carbon dioxide, a gas left over after your body uses the oxygen you breathe in.

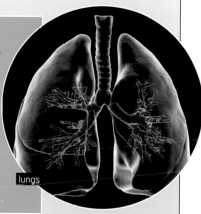
lungs

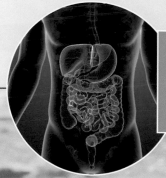

DIGESTIVE SYSTEM

Bon appétit! Your digestive system is what brings food—and its nutrients—into your body. It then turns the nutrients from food into energy. And it also gets rid of waste!

MUSCULAR SYSTEM

Muscles make you move! From walking and running to chewing and swallowing, muscles are responsible for your motion. Some muscles, such as your heart, are moving even when you aren't.

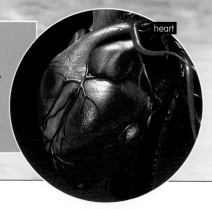
heart

WHY does PUBERTY HAPPEN?

Growing—whether it's getting tall enough to ride the scariest rides at an amusement park or turning old enough to stay up late—can seem to take forever. But there are two times in your life where you grow super quickly! The first of these is when you're a baby. The second is during puberty. Puberty happens when it's time for your body to start making the final physical changes from kid to adult. Your brain releases special hormones that will start to change different parts of your body. During puberty, many kids go through growth spurts, when they get taller very quickly. Other changes include ones in body hair, sweat production, voice tone, and the development of sexual organs. Because so many hormones are at work at once, puberty can also lead to lots of different emotions. But you're not alone: All animals transition from infants to adults!

SAY **WHAT?!**

SCIENTISTS THINK THAT YOUNG DOGS GO THROUGH AN EMOTIONAL "TEENAGE" PHASE JUST LIKE HUMANS!

During PUBERTY, KIDS can GROW as many as FOUR INCHES (10 cm) PER YEAR!

FOR INSECTS, THE CHANGE FROM YOUNG INSECT TO ADULT IS CALLED METAMORPHOSIS.

SAY **WHAT?!**

WHY do I have EYEBROWS?

We think we know why humans tend to not have much hair on our bodies (see p. 8). So why do we have *any* hair at all? And why is it in certain places? Eyebrows and eyelashes are easy to explain—they protect our eyes. Eyelashes keep things like dust, dirt, and water out of our eyes. Eyebrows block sunlight and direct sweat and rain away from our eyes. They also help us communicate through facial expressions and recognize each other. The reason for the hair on our heads and bodies is a bit trickier, though. Scientists think humans may have hairy heads to shield our scalps from the sun or possibly to keep us warmer at night. As for the hair in other places, such as in many adults' armpits, scientists think that *this* hair might protect the skin in sensitive places while we move. All in all— lots of hair, lots of reasons!

MANY PEOPLE HAVE A "DOMINANT EYEBROW"—ONE THAT IS EASIER TO MOVE THAN THE OTHER.

Hair Care Through History

Hair care is as ancient as humans are. The oldest type of grooming was first practiced by our ancient ancestors and is still around today: getting rid of parasites. Some animals, such as other primates, use their nimble fingers to pick lice and other parasites out of each other's fur. (In fact, this might be part of the reason humans developed fingernails.) Over the ages, people invented tools to help with this particular chore. Lice combs have been found around the world; some of the oldest are from 3,500 years ago. Humans also began to develop hairstyles. Some scientists even think that a figurine made nearly 30,000 years ago depicts a woman wearing braids! Hairstyles served many purposes, just like they do today. Both women and men wore different styles to protect their hair, to keep it out of the way, to show off their social status or tribal affiliation, and to look nice.

Some **ANCIENT ROMAN WOMEN DYED THEIR HAIR** using a mixture of **VINEGAR** and **ROTTEN LEECHES.**

vinegar

WHY do I have MUSCLES?

You have more than 600 muscles in your body, and they keep every single part of you moving! Muscles are a type of tissue made of thousands of stretchy fibers. There are three types of muscle: skeletal, cardiac, and smooth. All muscle types work by squeezing and relaxing, but they all have different jobs. Skeletal muscle is what you see when bodybuilders flex their arms. Many of these muscles are connected to your bones by tissues called tendons. Tendons let you and your body move by pushing and pulling on your skeleton whenever you want them to. That's right—you control them, whether you're using them to kick a ball or pet a dog. But cardiac muscle, which makes up your heart, and smooth muscles are moving whether you think about them or not. Smooth muscles help your organs, such as your stomach or bladder, work. So right now, even as you're reading this, you're using your muscles!

SAY WHAT?!

AN ELEPHANT'S TRUNK CONTAINS ABOUT 40,000 MUSCLES.

CATS **HAVE 32 MUSCLES** IN EACH EAR.

When you wear **MUSCLES** down during activity, your body **REBUILDS** them with **NEW CELLS.**

WHY do people have TWO EYES?

With all kinds of eyes in the animal kingdom, how is it that people ended up with just two forward-facing ones? The particular positioning of our peepers creates something called binocular vision, and it's pretty important for a lot of predators, humans included. Our eyes see at slightly different angles that overlap with each other. Our brains sort out images in ways that give us a three-dimensional view of what's in front of us, including the ability to judge depth, length, width, and distance. But why are our eyes on the front of our face? This is thanks to our ancestors, who had to rely on hunting to find food. When hunting prey, predators often find it easiest to track and move toward something in front of them (although there are exceptions). And as for having just two? In nature, simpler is often easier—more eyes would take a lot more energy to grow and manage—and a set of two has been working just fine for thousands of years!

IN BRIGHT LIGHT, CUTTLEFISH HAVE W-SHAPED PUPILS.

Eye Spy ...

Take this quiz on animal eyes and see if you can spot the right answers!

1. What land animal has the largest eyes?
a. elephant
b. ostrich
c. tarsier

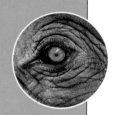

Scientists think that DOGS can see ULTRAVIOLET LIGHT, which HUMANS cannot.

2. Which animal can see all the way around itself without moving its head?
a. rabbit
b. horse
c. owl

3. Which animal has eyes that can each swivel around on their own?
a. honeybee
b. hammerhead shark
c. chameleon

4. Which animal has eyes directly on top of its head?
a. bat
b. flounder
c. giraffe

5. This animal has eight eyes and can see 100 times better than a human at night:
a. ogre-faced spider
b. cat
c. mantis shrimp

ANSWERS: 1. b; 2. a; 3. c; 4. b; 5. a

WHAT happens to the FOOD I EAT?

What happens to food after you swallow it? Actually, you start digesting your food *before* you even swallow. Saliva, or spit, has special substances called enzymes that start breaking down food the second it enters your mouth. After that, your tongue helps push your mashed-up mouthful to the back of your throat, where it enters a pipe called the esophagus. Muscles in your esophagus squeeze the food down toward your stomach. Once your meal is in your stomach, more muscles and something called gastric acid help turn the food into a liquid mush. The mush then enters the small intestine. Three of your organs—your liver, pancreas, and gallbladder—create juices that help your body absorb nutrients from the mush. The nutrients head to your liver to be absorbed, while the leftover waste mush moves on to your large intestine. And the last stop for the waste? It moves on to your colon, where it comes out as—you guessed it—poop!

SAY **WHAT?!**

THE PLATYPUS HAS NO STOMACH.

STRETCHED OUT, AN ADULT'S SMALL INTESTINE WOULD BE MORE THAN THREE TIMES AS LONG AS THE AVERAGE ADULT IS TALL!

IT CAN TAKE A SLOTH TWO WEEKS TO DIGEST A MEAL.

SAY **WHAT?!**

WHY do I BREATHE AIR?

DOLPHINS SLEEP UNDERWATER by SHUTTING DOWN HALF of their BRAIN at a time.

Taking air into your body is as natural as, well, breathing. You do it without thinking. But why do humans need air in the first place? Just like food is fuel for our bodies, air is fuel for our bodies' tiniest living units: our cells. Cells are microscopic and make up every part of us. Cells need a gas called oxygen to function and to produce energy for our bodies. To get oxygen to our cells, we rely on our respiratory system. When you take a deep breath, or inhale, you are pulling air—and oxygen—into your lungs. To inhale, your body uses a muscle called the diaphragm. As this muscle squeezes, it helps expand your lungs, pulling in air. The air moves from your nose or mouth down through a tube called the trachea and into your lungs, where it enters tiny air sacs called alveoli. From there, blood helps carry the oxygen through your circulatory system (see p. 10) to different parts of your body.

WHY can't
I hold my BREATH
LONGER?

On average, whales can hold their breath for about an hour. On the other hand, most humans can only hold their breath for about 30 seconds to two minutes. That's because humans just aren't built for it! When humans breathe in air, they store it in their lungs. When you hold your breath, it means that you are keeping the air in your lungs instead of breathing it back out. As you do this, your circulatory system is using up all the oxygen from the air inside your lungs and slowly leaving behind a waste gas called carbon dioxide. This means that humans can only hold their breath for as long as they can keep oxygen in their lungs. Unlike humans, whales store oxygen in their blood and their muscles. They can also slow down the functions of many of their organs, meaning that they use less oxygen over time.

The LONGEST recorded DIVE by a WHALE lasted for about THREE HOURS!

WHY do I have SO MANY ORGANS?

Each person has approximately 78 organs—more than 300 if you count each bone and tooth! We have so many because almost every organ does a different job. Some, such as your skin, are on the outside. Called the integumentary system, skin is your largest organ. It protects everything inside of you and helps keep out viruses and bacteria. Other organs, such as the kidneys and bladder, are on the inside. Kidneys clean your blood and turn liquid waste into urine, which is stored in your bladder (see p. 143). Many organs work together as part of a system. Your kidneys and bladder work as part of your urinary system. Another example is your digestive system. When you eat, your mouth, esophagus, stomach, liver, intestines, and more all perform different jobs in order to process food and deliver nutrients to your body (see p. 26). Your organs all work together to keep your body healthy.

The CHINESE SOFT-SHELLED TURTLE PEES from its MOUTH.

SAY WHAT?!

BECAUSE THE GLASS FROG'S SKIN IS SEE-THROUGH, YOU CAN SEE ITS HEART!

SAY **WHAT?!**

SCIENTISTS THINK THAT CEPHALOPODS MIGHT BE ABLE TO SENSE LIGHT WITH THEIR SKIN.

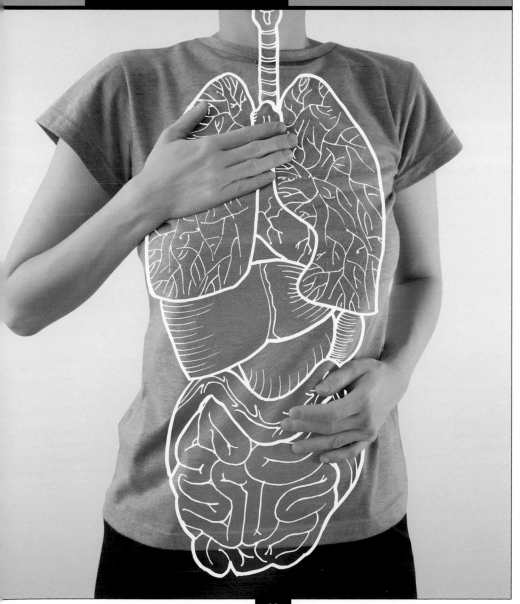

WHY do I BLUSH?

From running around on hot summer days to embarrassing moments, you may have noticed your skin start to turn red at certain times. Often called flushing or blushing, this redness can happen for different reasons. After you've been playing hard, your body temperature tends to get higher. One way your body keeps cool is to sweat (see p. 50), but another is to expand your blood vessels to let more oxygen flow through your body. This causes the blood to rush toward the surface of your skin, cooling it off ... and turning you red! Another reason for the redness is your emotions. When you are embarrassed, nervous, or extra excited, your body often releases a hormone called adrenaline. Just like heat, adrenaline causes your blood vessels to expand and blood to rush toward your skin. But why? Scientists think blushing may have developed as a form of wordless communication.

WHEN YOU BLUSH, THE LINING OF YOUR STOMACH ALSO TURNS RED.

SOME BLUSH MAKEUP CONTAINS A DYE MADE FROM CRUSHED-UP INSECTS.

Blushing
Birds

For hundreds of years, people thought that humans were the only animals that blush. But scientists discovered that birds blush, too! From crested caracaras to vultures, the skin around the eyes, beak, or nape of the neck of

vultures

many kinds of birds will flush when they feel strong emotions. To understand this better, scientists conducted a study on macaw parrots. They found that—just like humans—blushing seems to occur in parrots as a way to help them communicate. Communicate what, exactly? Scientists aren't sure yet!

PEOPLE don't start BLUSHING until they are TWO to THREE YEARS OLD.

WHY don't I HAVE a TAIL?

Actually, humans *do* have tails! As they are developing in the womb, humans have a tail for a very short time. Once they are born, all that's left of that tail is the tailbone. So when it comes to tails, why did humans get the short end of the stick, so to speak? Animals that spend all or most of their time on all fours or in the water tend to have tails to help them stay balanced. For example, cheetahs use their tails to balance and turn quickly when they run. But as human ancestors slowly began to walk upright over the years, they no longer needed help balancing. In fact, a tail would just get in the way when walking on two feet. So over time, the tails of human ancestors got shorter and shorter—until they disappeared altogether.

RED PANDAS often use their PLUSH TAILS as BLANKETS in cold weather.

WHY do humans **WALK** on **TWO LEGS?**

Human ancestors evolved from walking on all fours to walking upright on just two legs. Scientists have several theories as to why. Many of them believe that human ancestors began to rely on their two hind legs to save energy. Walking on two legs uses less energy than walking on four, which means that humans can do more activities while eating less food. Walking on two legs instead of four also would have freed up our ancestors' hands to carry more food or to use tools more easily. Other scientists think that standing on two legs would have helped humans see over tall grasses to hunt and to avoid other predators. Or it could have helped our ancestors stay cool, since walking upright means that less of your body is exposed to the hot sun.

Scientists think that some **DINOSAURS** developed TINY **ARMS** to help them **BALANCE** on two legs.

WHY can't I SEE in the DARK?

Why is it that cats can see in the dark, but humans can't? The answer has a lot to do with the shape of our eyes. To see, humans rely on light bouncing off the objects around us (see p. 39). This light enters our eyes through round openings called pupils. After that, the light hits special cells in the back of our eyes that send signals to our brain to create images. But when it is dark, there is less light to enter our eyes and hit these cells. It becomes harder for us to see nearby objects and to process color. Cats, on the other hand, have eyes that can let in much more light. Not only do they have a special reflective structure in their eyes called a tapetum lucidum, but they also have slit-shaped pupils that can expand more than ours can.

Night Vision Tech

Humans may not be able to see very well in the dark on their own, but that doesn't mean that they can't see in the dark at all! Thanks to some amazing technology, humans have found ways to create their own artificial night vision. One type of technology, often called image enhancement, captures existing light and then magnifies it to create a much brighter image on a screen. Image enhancement is often used when making night vision goggles. Another type of night vision technology uses infrared light, a form of energy that humans can't see but can feel as heat. Some cameras can see infrared light and then convert it to an image for the human eye.

EAGLES can see more than FOUR TIMES FARTHER than humans can.

SNAKES CAN SEE INFRARED LIGHT.

WHY CAN'T I STARE AT THE SUN?

You've probably heard it all your life: Don't look directly at the sun. But why? Well, your eyes are a lot more sensitive than your skin (though your skin still needs protection with the help of things such as sunscreen). To understand why direct sunlight can be harmful to your eyes, let's take a closer look at how eyes work.

PUPIL
The pupil is the dark circle in the center of your eye. It lets in light.

IRIS
The colored part of your eye is called the iris. The iris helps control how much light enters your eye.

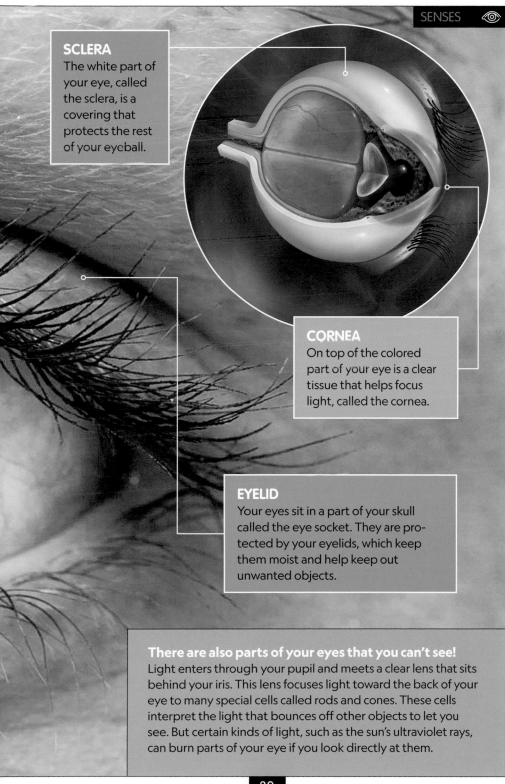

SCLERA

The white part of your eye, called the sclera, is a covering that protects the rest of your eyeball.

CORNEA

On top of the colored part of your eye is a clear tissue that helps focus light, called the cornea.

EYELID

Your eyes sit in a part of your skull called the eye socket. They are protected by your eyelids, which keep them moist and help keep out unwanted objects.

There are also parts of your eyes that you can't see!

Light enters through your pupil and meets a clear lens that sits behind your iris. This lens focuses light toward the back of your eye to many special cells called rods and cones. These cells interpret the light that bounces off other objects to let you see. But certain kinds of light, such as the sun's ultraviolet rays, can burn parts of your eye if you look directly at them.

WHY do I SHIVER?

Brrr ... who turned down the heat? To function, your body needs to stay within a certain temperature range. While the average body temperature is about 98.6°F (37°C), healthy temperatures can range from 97° to 99°F (36.1° to 37.2°C). When your body gets too cold, it tries to warm itself up. One of the ways it does this is by shivering. Muscles throughout your body quickly alternate between squeezing and relaxing. This creates energy, which gives off a little bit of heat. Shivering is an involuntary reaction, which means that it happens without your control. Goose bumps are also an involuntary reaction. When you are cold, small muscles in your skin contract and release to create warmth. This makes your hair follicles—the places where your soft body hair grows—stand up, trapping a layer of warming air between your hair and your body.

SAY WHAT?!

WOLVES HAVE TWO LAYERS OF FUR THAT KEEP THEM WARM IN THE SNOW.

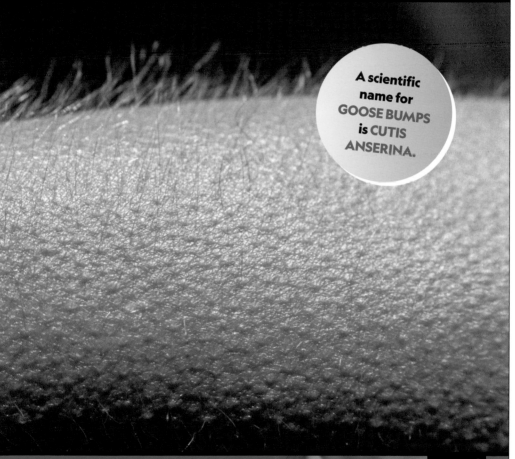

A scientific name for GOOSE BUMPS is CUTIS ANSERINA.

WOOD FROGS SURVIVE BY FREEZING DURING THE WINTER. THEY STOP BREATHING AND THEIR HEART STOPS BEATING.

SAY WHAT?!

CAN
I TASTE every
FLAVOR?

Many scientists have labeled five basic tastes that humans can detect: sweet, salty, bitter, sour, and savory. You can identify these tastes through organs on your tongue called taste buds. Have you ever noticed that your tongue is covered in tiny bumps? These bumps, called papillae, are where your taste buds live. Taste buds have microscopic hairs that, when they come into contact with a flavor, send signals to your brain that allow you to taste things. Scientists think that we developed the ability to taste in order to recognize nutrient-rich foods and avoid foods that would make us sick. But are these five tastes the only flavors out there? Not necessarily! Some scientists think that other tastes—such as calcium, spiciness, and fat—count as their own flavors. There might even be flavors out there that humans can't taste at all!

IT IS A MYTH THAT YOU TASTE DIFFERENT FLAVORS WITH DIFFERENT PARTS OF YOUR TONGUE.

Taste Test

CATS can't taste SWEET things.

Consider yourself a foodie? Take this just-for-fun quiz to test your sense smarts!

1. About how many taste buds does each person have on average?
a. 100
b. one million
c. 10,000

2. True or False: Your taste buds for different tastes are located in different sections of your tongue.

3. What is your sense of taste called?
a. gustatory system
b. palate system
c. flavor system

4. Which substance in your mouth helps digest food?
a. papillae
b. gums
c. saliva

5. True or False: Your sense of taste changes as you get older.

ANSWERS: 1. c, 2. false, 3. a, 4. c, 5. true

WHY do I like SWEET and SALTY THINGS?

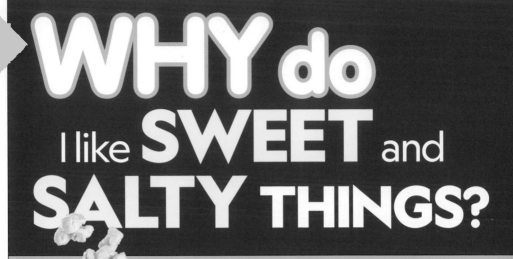

It's snack time! Do you reach for the salty treat or the sweet one? You might want both! But eating too much of foods that contain tons of sugar or salt can be bad for your health. So why do we crave them? The answer goes all the way back to our prehuman primate ancestors who lived high up in the trees. Both sugar and salt are important for human survival. Our bodies need them to function and to make energy. But even though sugary fruits might have been available up in the trees, they wouldn't have been super plentiful, and salt would have been very tough to find. Cravings made sure that primate ancestors would search for foods that contained these ingredients. Some foods, like fruit, had the added bonus of also providing water. Today, both salty and sweet foods are much easier to get our hands on ... but that doesn't mean we want them any less!

SOME BUTTERFLIES DRINK ANIMAL URINE FOR THE MINERALS IT CONTAINS.

Some scientists think that **PEOPLE** who have **MORE TASTE BUDS** may tend to **PREFER SALTY** foods over **SWEET** ones.

SOME MOUNTAIN GOATS LICK ROCKS TO GET THE SALT THEY NEED.

HOW do I FEEL THINGS?

Whether something is soft, rough, or smooth, you can sense it by feeling it with your skin. You have this ability thanks to your nervous system. The nervous system controls many activities such as walking and breathing. It also allows you to interact with the world by feeling things. This system includes your brain (see p. 102), spinal cord, and nerves. Nerves are long groups of fibers that send messages to your brain through your spinal cord, which is made up of nerve tissue protected by your backbone. Every nerve that runs from your brain down through your spinal cord has a place where it stops: a nerve ending. Many nerve endings are in your skin. When nerve endings come in contact with an object, they send electrical signals to your brain. Your brain then interprets this information as feeling. This helps you understand the world better, as well as avoid dangerous items that are hot or sharp.

Super Senses

Just like you, almost all animals can feel the world around them through their nervous system. But for some animals, this is not their most important—or coolest— way of interacting with the world.

Sharks have a small line of holes near their snout. These are actually a special organ called the ampullae of Lorenzini, and they allow a shark to sense electric signals. Many types of marine animals give off small amounts of electricity. This means that sharks can use their ampullae of Lorenzini to track down meals.

Other animals also have unique ways of sensing the world. Many different kinds of animals, such as dogs, sea turtles, cows, and birds, can sense Earth's magnetic fields. Some animals, such as red foxes, use these magnetic fields to hunt prey. Others, such as sea turtles and birds, may use this sense to navigate.

Research shows that TOUCHING SOFT THINGS can COMFORT PEOPLE.

SOME SCIENTISTS THINK THAT THE BACTERIA IN AN ANIMAL'S BODY ARE WHAT ENABLE IT TO SENSE MAGNETIC FIELDS.

WHY do I get ITCHY?

Dry skin, mosquitoes, poison ivy—a lot of things cause itches. Itching may seem like just a nuisance, but a lot is actually happening in your body when you itch—and this feeling exists for a reason. You have bundles of fibers called nerves (see p. 42) all over your body. When the ends of these fibers, called nerve endings, touch something, they send messages to your brain that let you feel whatever it is you're touching. Inside your skin, you also have special nerve endings called pruriceptors. When activated, these pruriceptors are specially designed to make you feel itchy. But why? Itchy skin is your body's way of letting you know that something might be irritating your skin, such as a rash-causing plant or bug. The itch draws your attention to the area so that you can hopefully swat—or scratch—whatever is bothering it.

SAY WHAT?!

DEER CAN EAT POISON IVY WITHOUT ITCHING.

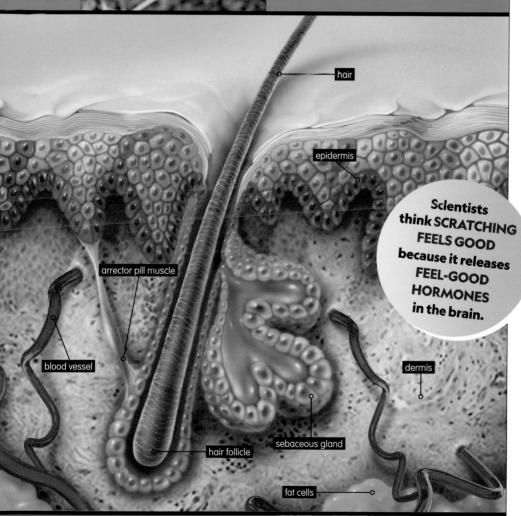

hair

epidermis

arrector pill muscle

blood vessel

Scientists think **SCRATCHING FEELS GOOD** because it releases **FEEL-GOOD HORMONES** in the brain.

dermis

hair follicle

sebaceous gland

fat cells

BEARS OFTEN SCRATCH ITCHES BY RUBBING THEIR BACKS AGAINST TREES.

SAY WHAT?!

WHAT happens when I get TOO HOT?

Your body has lots of ways of staying cool. When you get too hot, your brain sends a message to special glands—a type of organ—that cause you to sweat. Sweat is made of water and chemicals and leaves your body through tiny openings in your skin called pores. Once sweat is on your skin, it starts to evaporate in the heat, meaning it turns from a liquid into a gas. In the process, it takes some of your heat with it, cooling you down. But what if your body touches something that's too hot? When your body's tissue comes into contact with a very hot item, it can get damaged. This is called a burn. Luckily, your body also has ways of protecting you. These include the instant reactions that make you pull back quickly when the marshmallow you're roasting—and the hand holding it on a stick!—get too close to the fire.

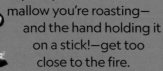

HIPPOS SWEAT A PINK LIQUID TO STAY COOL.

Beat the Heat

Not all animals sweat to stay cool—in fact, most don't! Check out the amazing ways these animals stay nice and comfortable.

Some types of birds, such as puffins, stay cool thanks to their large beaks. When a puffin gets too hot, the heat can escape through its large bill.

Other birds, like vultures, have an, ahem, slightly messier way of beating the heat. They poop on themselves! This liquid poop acts kind of like sweat in that it evaporates over time, taking some heat with it.

Also messy? Wallowing in mud! Animals such as pigs don't have a natural way to sweat. Instead, they roll around in mud, which cools them off as the water evaporates from the dirt.

Elephants have a much more elegant solution: They flap their large ears like fans.

HUMANS have between TWO and FOUR MILLION SWEAT GLANDS.

WHY do humans HEAR?

For almost all animals—humans included—hearing is an important sense for survival. The ability to hear noises lets animals know that something is approaching and alerts them to possible danger. It also helps them identify when important things are nearby, such as prey or water. But for humans especially, hearing has served another purpose: communication. Sound lets people share information even in situations where they cannot see one another. So how does hearing work? For humans, hearing takes place in the outer and inner ears. Sound waves travel first to a person's outer ear—the part you see. Then, vibrations in a thin tissue called the eardrum pass sound to the middle ear. The sound is then magnified by tiny ear bones before traveling to the inner ear. Small cells called hair cells work to translate the sound into electrical messages, which are then sent to the brain.

SNAKES HEAR through their JAWBONES.

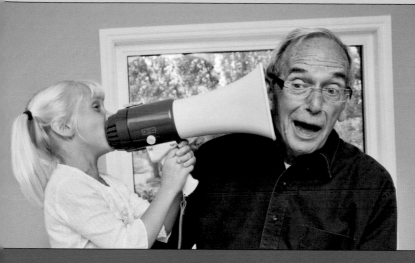

WHY can I HEAR BETTER than GROWN-UPS can?

Have you ever had a favorite shirt that you wore over and over again? Did you notice that after a while, it started to become a little more worn? The same thing can happen to adults' ears! After years of hearing sounds, the small, delicate hair cells in the inner ear can start to get worn out. This means that it will not be as easy for them to hear some sounds. These same cells can also be damaged by listening to very loud music or hearing extra loud noises. Does that mean that kids can hear better than adults? In general, yes! Most kids have hair cells that are fresher and less worn than those of adults, meaning that they can hear things adults no longer can. In fact, kids not only hear better—they can also hear certain tones that are too high-pitched for adult ears!

Scientists think ELEPHANTS might be able to HEAR STORMS as far as 150 MILES (241 km) AWAY.

LEGENDS OF THE
SIXTH SENSE

For centuries, people have wondered if some humans might have a sense beyond the basic five of sight, sound, hearing, taste, and touch. Various theories held that a "sixth sense" might include mind reading, moving things with your mind, the ability to tell the future, and more. These abilities have since been debunked, for the most part (see p. 118). But could there be something beyond our five senses?

SOME SCIENTISTS THINK OUR HUMAN ANCESTORS COULD SENSE ELECTRICAL SIGNALS LIKE SHARKS DO.

THE REAL SIXTH SENSE

Many scientists now say that humans do have a sixth sense: the ability to tell where all our body parts are in space without looking at them. This very real sixth sense is called proprioception. It means that you can easily use your limbs in the dark, touch your finger to your nose without thinking about it, and understand how to interact with objects around you.

MORE SENSES

OK, so what about a seventh sense ... or an eighth? Scientists think some humans might have those too, or that we might one day develop them. One of these abilities, which some people may already have, is the ability to detect Earth's magnetic fields. Birds, foxes, and other animals can use these magnetic fields to get around (see p. 47) and some scientists are studying whether humans can as well!

Other scientists think that humans might even be able to develop the ability to get around like bats and dolphins do. This sense, known as echolocation, lets some animals navigate by bouncing noises off objects and listening for the echoes to return. Scientists are studying people who may have learned to echolocate to determine whether other humans could learn to do that as well.

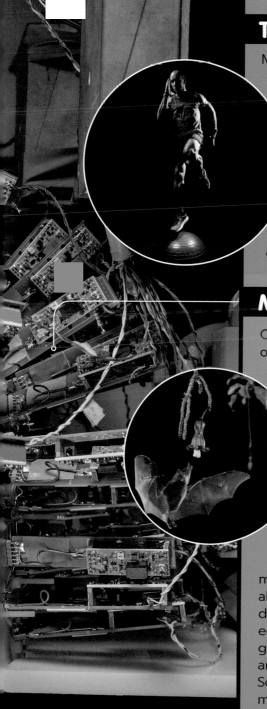

An engineer wears a helmet of sensors, which is part of a brain scanner.

WHY do some SMELLS STINK?

Chances are your favorite smell isn't a big pile of dog poo or the scent of skunk spray. We think certain things stink because recognizing a smelly substance helps keep us safe. Scents are made up of an object's teeny-tiny molecules. These molecules travel through the air and enter through your nose when you breathe. In the top inside area of your nose, you have special cells called olfactory sensory neurons. These cells are designed to respond to the molecules they encounter by sending messages to your brain. Your brain then interprets these messages as smells. When your brain interprets a molecule as a "bad" smell, it is usually warning you to stay away. Over time, humans have evolved to find the scents of harmful items—such as rotten food or bacteria-filled poop—repulsive. This is why items that could make you sick often smell so bad.

The Smelliest Things on Earth

There sure are a lot of stinky scents in the world—but which is the worst? According to scientists, these are some of the foulest stenches.

DURIAN

Found across Southeast Asia, this spiky fruit with a soft center is known for its pungent odor. Although many people find the taste pleasing, the fruit is said to reek of rotting meat, sewage, and gym socks.

SEAL ISLAND

One of the worst-smelling places on Earth may be this tiny island off the coast of South Africa. Home to tens of thousands of fur seals, the island smells of rotting fish and fishy seal poop!

URANUS

OK, so it's not on Earth, but Uranus really reeks! According to scientists, the planet's atmosphere is chock-full of hydrogen sulfide—the same chemical that gives rotten eggs their smell.

The same chemical is responsible for the way both PARMESAN CHEESE and VOMIT smell.

HYDROGEN SULFIDE CAN ALSO BE FOUND IN THE GAS PEOPLE PASS.

WHY do SCENTS jog my MEMORY?

Does the scent of sunscreen make you think of your favorite summer days? Or maybe the smell of your favorite meal reminds you of a family member? For years, people have known that scents can trigger certain memories, but they haven't known exactly why. Now scientists are learning that the reason smell and memory are so connected is related to our brain anatomy (see p. 100). Scents travel through the same places in our brain that process memories and emotions. This can link the two together so that when you inhale a certain scent, any memories associated with it are also triggered inside your brain. There's even a name for this occurrence: the Proust effect.

A BLOOD-HOUND'S EARS help it SEND SCENTS up toward its nose.

Some DOGS can pick up SCENTS more than 12 MILES (20 km) AWAY.

WHY can't I SMELL as WELL as a DOG CAN?

Dogs have an amazing sense of smell—in fact, scientists think that some dogs can smell 100,000 times better than a human. There are a few reasons for a dog's super sniffer. High inside our human noses, we have tons of tiny, special cells that are designed to react to scent molecules (see p. 56). These cells are called olfactory receptors. Humans have about six million of these receptors. Dogs, on the other hand, have up to 300 million!

A dog's nose is also built very differently. While humans breathe in and out through the same airway, dogs breathe in through each nostril separately. When breathing out, dogs exhale through the flat slits on the sides of their nose. This lets them hold on to scents longer. Dogs also have a special organ for sniffing. Called Jacobson's organ, it can detect hormones, which humans can't smell.

WHY does MUSIC make me MOVE?

Your favorite song comes on, and you just have to get up and dance—but why? The short answer: Dancing to music makes us happy! Scientists aren't sure why certain collections of noise—aka music—that enter our ears make us want to move. But they do have some ideas. Scientists studying music have discovered that it acts on more parts of our brain than just the ones that interpret sound. Music activates parts of our brain that trigger happiness as well. Some of these "happiness areas" are also connected to parts of the brain that control movement. On top of that, music directly stimulates a different part of our brain that relates to movement and coordination. As for reasons beyond those, scientists are still figuring it out. In the meantime, keep dancing!

SCIENTISTS HAVE TRAINED GRAY SEALS TO COPY HUMAN WORDS AND SONGS.

SAY WHAT?!

SAY **WHAT?!**

JUST LIKE HUMANS, PARROTS SEEM TO LOVE TO DANCE.

Studies show that DANCING can IMPROVE a PERSON'S MOOD and REDUCE STRESS.

WHY do SOUR FOODS

make my mouth PUCKER?

Whenever someone bites or licks a lemon, there's a good chance they'll have a strong reaction. Their eyes might close, their face might scrunch up, and their mouth will probably start to water. The same goes for any other super sour food or candy. It turns out that your body is not so great at recognizing different kinds of sour foods. Most sour foods are high in something called acidity. Some things that are acidic are harmful to humans or poisonous. Of course, lemons and many other sour foods are usually very safe for people to eat. But your body doesn't know this, so when you eat sour foods, your taste buds send a warning signal to your brain. Your mouth will produce more saliva to help get rid of the acidity, and your face will often scrunch up as part of a warning your brain sends to your body.

THERE IS A BERRY IN WESTERN AFRICA THAT, WHEN EATEN, CAN MAKE SOUR THINGS TASTE SWEET!

62

Trick Your Taste Buds

PINEAPPLE is not only ACIDIC; it contains a SUBSTANCE that actually BREAKS DOWN the things it touches.

Sour foods aren't the only things that can confuse your taste buds. Try these fun tricks to hack your taste buds!

SWEET SIPPING

Artichokes contain a chemical that sticks to the sweet taste cells on your tongue. When you drink water right after eating artichokes, the chemical activates the sensation of sweetness!

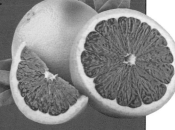

GREAT GRAPEFRUIT

If you find a grapefruit a bit too bitter, try adding ... salt! It seems strange, but salt on grapefruit blocks the bitter chemicals from reaching your tongue, leaving behind more sweetness.

TASTE-BE-GONE

If you have to swallow something you don't like, try holding your nose. Our senses of taste and smell are linked, so this trick blocks most of the flavor. (Just make sure not to be rude about it!)

WHY do COLD THINGS hurt my TEETH?

Just the thought of biting into an ice-cream bar or a snow cone might make you shiver. If so, you're not alone. For lots of people, eating or drinking something too cold can cause a strange, somewhat unpleasant feeling in their teeth. This has to do with a tooth's anatomy. Each of your teeth is made up of a tough material called dentin. Surrounding the dentin is a hard coating, called enamel, which protects your teeth from wear and tear. At the very center of your tooth is a fleshy tissue called pulp. Your tooth's pulp is home to nerve endings and blood vessels. It also ends in a root that secures the tooth into your jawbone. When you bite into something too cold—or hot— that little twinge you feel is when the nerve endings in this pulp send an alert to your brain.

diagram of tooth

GOATS DON'T HAVE UPPER FRONT TEETH.

SAY WHAT?!

SAY WHAT?!

YOU CAN TELL A DOLPHIN'S AGE BY ITS TEETH.

According to one survey, **26 PERCENT** of **PEOPLE PREFER TO BITE** into their **ICE CREAM.**

WHAT are GENES?

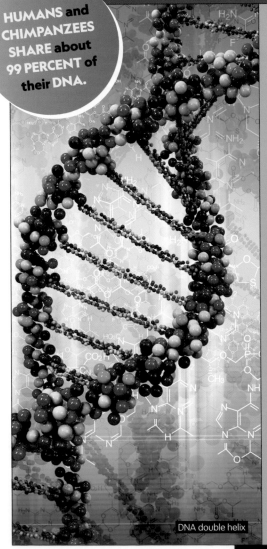

DNA double helix

In each of your cells, you have microscopic threadlike structures called chromosomes. These chromosomes are made up of something called DNA, or deoxyribonucleic acid. DNA is found in every single living thing, from a tiny fruit fly to an enormous elephant. In your chromosomes, DNA is grouped into units. Each unit acts as the instructions for making a protein. Larger sections of these units are called genes. Proteins are your body's building blocks, and your genes tell the proteins what to build and how. Genes determine how your body functions and how it grows. They also influence some of the things that make you *you*. This includes how you look—from your hair color to your eye color to your height—how you act, some of the things you like ... and so much more! Many of the things that genes influence are known as traits.

If uncoiled, all the **DNA** from just **ONE** of your **CELLS** would stretch about **SIX FEET** (2 m).

WHERE do GENES COME FROM?

Genes come from your biological parents. So if someone ever tells you that you have your biological parent's eyes, they mean their genes! In humans, each cell usually contains 46 chromosomes. These chromosomes come in pairs. This means that each cell usually has 23 pairs of chromosomes. In each pair of chromosomes, one chromosome comes from the male parent and the other from the female. One pair of chromosomes determines the biological sex of the child. The rest of the pairs contain the genes for the traits that you have, such as whether or not you have freckles, what your facial features look like, or even whether you like spicy foods. Since one half of the pair comes from each parent, you might look more like your biological mother or more like your biological father—or you might look like both! Your genes might also combine in surprising ways (see p. 72) that make you look different from either parent.

ANATOMY OF **DNA**

DNA is microscopic, but it makes us who we are. What exactly does it look like? DNA is made from chemical substances that are joined together in a shape called a double helix. This double helix is made of two long strands of chemicals that are connected by shorter strands in the middle, like a ladder. The whole shape is then twisted. Take a look at this diagram to get a peek at the tiny structures that make you *you!*

HUMANS CONTAIN DNA FROM RELATED PRIMATE SPECIES THAT ARE NOW EXTINCT.

CELL
The cell is your body's smallest living unit. Cells make up all of your body's tissues. Chromosomes are found inside your cells.

ALL DNA IS MADE OF JUST FOUR BASES.

CHROMOSOME
Chromosomes are threadlike structures, made of DNA, that hold all the instructions that determine how your body will look and function.

GENE
Each section of DNA that contains a full code for a specific protein is called a gene.

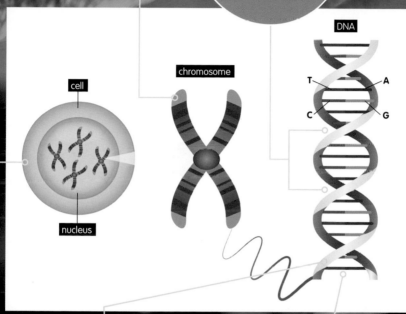

cell

nucleus

chromosome

DNA

T   A

C   G

BACKBONE
DNA is supported by two structural strands, or backbones, made of chemicals. These make the "rails" of the ladder shape.

BASE PAIRS
Molecules known as bases are attached to the backbone of each DNA strand. Each molecule attaches to another molecule on the opposite backbone, forming a base pair. These make the "rungs" of the ladder shape. The order of these base pairs holds the code for your genes.

WHY does everyone look DIFFERENT?

From height to coloring to facial features and more, humans around the world look different in all kinds of ways. But how is this possible when humans are about 99.6 percent genetically alike? First, humans have a lot of genes: some 20,000 to 25,000, to be specific. Second, genes can combine in many different ways. In fact, some scientists estimate that there are more than 70 trillion possible combinations of genes. That means that there are trillions more potential gene combinations than the number of people who ever lived! But why is it that we can—and do—look so different? After all, many animals look a lot more alike than humans do. According to scientists, this has to do with how social humans are. Because we tend to interact with each other so much, it was helpful for us to evolve to be more easily recognizable.

Animal Analysis

Just like us, animals rely on their senses to recognize one another. But for many animals, sight plays a less important role. According to scientists, lots of animals rely most on smell and hearing to know what's next to them. Dogs in particular are great at recognizing scents (see p. 59). Other animals, such as birds, can recognize distinct calls and cries to find their way back to their young.

So how do animals recognize humans? It depends! Research has shown that cats likely rely most on sound, scent, and touch to identify people. Dogs, meanwhile, have evolved alongside humans to not only recognize individual faces, but to read facial expressions as well. And in one study, scientists found that sheep could recognize people just by their pictures!

ONE STUDY FOUND THAT CATS CAN TELL RECORDINGS OF THEIR OWNERS' VOICES APART FROM THOSE OF OTHERS.

HOW can FAMILY MEMBERS look so DIFFERENT?

chromosome

Have you ever noticed that while some biological siblings look a lot alike, others don't? Even though two people are genetically related, one might have naturally curly hair while the other has naturally straight hair. This might seem surprising. After all, their genes come from the same parents. However, that doesn't mean they share all the exact same genes! Imagine one set of parents: Each of their biological children receives 23 pairs of chromosomes. Each pair has one half from the male parent and one half from the female. This means that for every gene on a pair of chromosomes, you have two sets of the gene—one from each parent. These sets are known as alleles. However, because your biological parents also have two sets of each gene, the alleles you receive might be different from what a sibling receives. And different combinations of alleles might make different traits, such as curly versus straight hair, appear.

SAY WHAT?!

SOMEONE WHO LOOKS ALMOST EXACTLY LIKE YOU BUT IS NOT BIOLOGICALLY RELATED IS CALLED A DOPPELGÄNGER.

As a result of GENETICS, all CALICO CATS are FEMALE.

SAY WHAT?!

SCIENTISTS HAVE FOUND HUMAN DNA ON A 5,700-YEAR-OLD PIECE OF TREE RESIN THAT WAS USED AS CHEWING GUM.

WHY do MOSQUITOES BITE ME?

Keep getting bitten by those pesky pests? Your genetics might be to blame! Scientists have held many theories over the years about why mosquitoes might be more drawn to some people than others. Some theories have included bacteria on your skin or even the color of your shirt. But now scientists think there might be a new culprit: your very own genes. Researchers believe that mosquitoes are most likely drawn to the way that certain people smell. And they think that this scent could be controlled by a person's genes. In fact, scientists estimate that about 20 percent of people are extra delicious to mosquitoes. They also believe that the way your body responds to a bite—including how itchy you get—might be based on your genes as well. Scientists don't have the complete picture yet, but they hope that the information they do have could lead to new ways of warding off the winged attackers.

ONLY FEMALE MOSQUITOES FEED ON BLOOD.

74

Dinosaur DNA

In one popular movie series, scientists bring dinosaurs back to life by creating clones from dino DNA. They get this DNA from dinosaur blood, millions of years old, that was found inside a fossilized mosquito. Is this at all possible? Right now, no. In the future? Maybe!

The first trick is finding a mosquito that has not only been fossilized with a bloody meal still in its belly, but one that lived during the time of the dinosaurs. (Scientists have found a blood-carrying fossilized mosquito from about 46 million years ago, but none from when dinosaurs lived ... yet.)

The next step is to successfully extract DNA from the insect. Scientists would then need to have the technology to clone animals, which is currently far from perfect (see p. 86). So bringing back your favorite dinosaur from a mosquito is still very unlikely ... but not entirely impossible!

One TYPE OF SPIDER that HUNTS MOSQUITOES is ATTRACTED to the smell of STINKY FEET.

IN 2020, SCIENTISTS WERE ABLE TO TAKE DNA FROM BEETLES THAT HAD BEEN FROZEN IN SAP, BUT THESE BEETLES HAD ONLY BEEN FROZEN FOR ABOUT SIX YEARS.

WHY can my HAIR CHANGE? as I grow

For lots of kids, hair changes as they get older, whether that's from light to dark, from curly to straight, or the opposite. Some of this has to do with your genes! Genes aren't always active. In fact, they can be turned on and off. This ability often helps your body make sure each part of it is functioning as it should, and that each of your cells is doing its individual job at the right time. This process is known as gene regulating. Sometimes, gene regulating can also affect how fast you grow and when (see p. 18). It can also affect the genes that control your appearance. A gene for curly hair might be turned on—or off—as you get older. Similarly, for lots of people, the genes that control darker pigments in their hair might turn on as they grow up.

DALMATIANS ARE BORN WITHOUT SPOTS.

Cat Match

Humans aren't the only animals with gene regulation. Try matching these kitten breeds with their adult versions. Thanks to gene regulation, it might be tougher than you think!

GENE REGULATION causes some COLD-WEATHER ANIMALS, such as arctic hares, to TURN WHITE in the WINTER.

SCOTTISH FOLD

EGYPTIAN MAU

SIAMESE

A

B

C

ANSWERS: A. Egyptian mau; B. Siamese; C. Scottish fold

CAN GENES CHANGE?

Genes sometimes turn "on" or "off" in order to function at different times. As people age, the ways these genes turn on or off sometimes changes as well. For the most part, the DNA that makes up your genes stays the same for your entire life. However, there are certain instances in which the DNA itself actually changes. For a long time, most scientists referred to these changes as mutations. These changes can happen when your cells, which are almost always copying themselves, make a mistake when copying the DNA they contain. A mutation can also happen if a person is exposed to certain chemicals or radiation. Sometimes, these changes can lead to health problems. Other times, they do not. Scientists now often refer to these mutations as genetic variants.

One **GENE VARIANT** can cause **CHEETAHS** to be **STRIPED** instead of spotted.

COULD
GENES give me
POWERS?

In comics and the movies, "mutated" genes—whether you're born with them, get them from a spider bite, or fall into a vat of radioactive ooze—can give you superpowers. Could that really happen? Well, you're almost certainly not going to start slinging spider webs or shooting lasers from your eyes. But gene variants can give people abilities that others don't have. Scientists have discovered a certain gene variant that lets muscles squeeze much more quickly. People who have this variant are often able to run faster than those who don't, or they may be able to lift more weight with less training. Another variant causes a person's bones to be extra strong. And yet another makes some people feel more rested on less sleep. Captain SuperSleep, anyone?

Long ago, SNAKES had TINY LEGS. GENE VARIANTS made them LEGLESS.

CAN I CHANGE my GENES?

So let's say you're tired of waiting to get taller, or you'd like to try out a different eye color for a while. Can you change your genes yourself? Or can you force your genes to turn on or off? Short answer, no. There is such a thing as gene changing but only for certain animals! Some cephalopods, such as squid and octopuses, can change their genes. While these animals don't change their DNA, they do change something very similar: RNA. Because DNA is so precious, it never leaves its safe home. Instead, it sends a copy—RNA—to move throughout the cell and create new proteins. By editing their RNA, cephalopods can change which protein will be made at a certain time. Scientists think this not only helped these animals get smarter, but it could also help them adapt quickly to different situations.

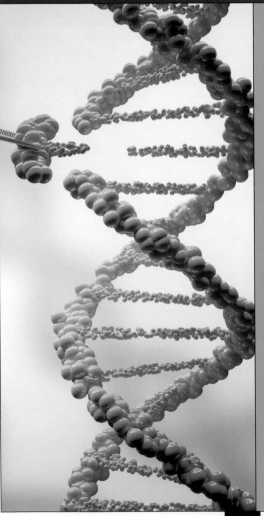

CHAMELEONS USE SPECIAL CELLS—NOT GENE EDITING—TO CHANGE COLORS.

SCIENTISTS are creating ways to EDIT GENES to help TREAT certain DISEASES.

SAY WHAT?!

USING GENE-EDITING TECHNOLOGY, SCIENTISTS BRED A SQUID THAT IS COMPLETELY SEE-THROUGH.

WHY do I LIKE some FOODS others don't?

Your friend takes a bite of a taco piled high with cilantro and makes a face—but you take a bite and squeal with delight. What gives? Much of our tastes in food were passed down from our human ancestors ages ago (see p. 44), so it can be surprising that we don't all share the same likes and dislikes when it comes to what's on our plate. Some food preferences have to do with what foods you grew up eating. But other tastes are in your genes. Scientists have discovered genetic variants that turn people into "super tasters." These people have taste buds that are much more sensitive. That means that certain things either taste differently to them or that they can taste some flavors more strongly. For example, some people have a gene that makes cilantro taste like soap. And for other people, celery tastes extremely bitter. Oh well—more cilantro for you!

SAY WHAT?!

SOME PEOPLE HAVE A GENE THAT MAKES THEM UNABLE TO SMELL APPLES.

Scientists think that a **PERSON'S ABILITY** to **ENJOY SPICY FOODS** might be partly **GENETIC.**

PENGUINS CAN TASTE ONLY SALTY OR SOUR FLAVORS.

SAY WHAT?!

WHAT ELSE
DO GENES INFLUENCE?

Genes influence what you look like and how sensitive your taste buds are. But can they influence other things in your life, too? Absolutely! Take a look at some of the stranger things that your genes affect.

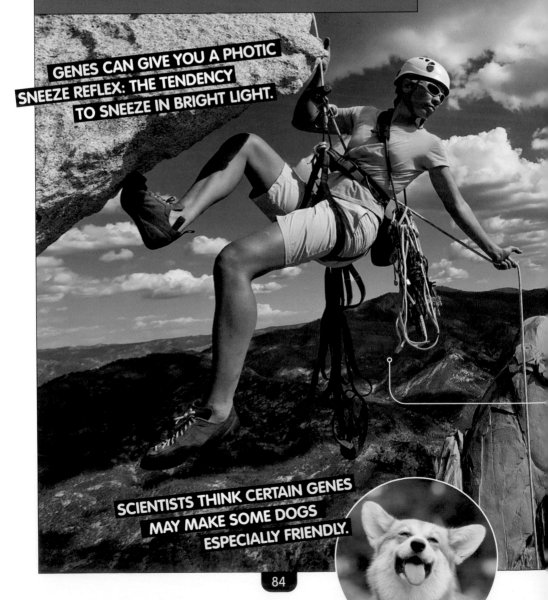

GENES CAN GIVE YOU A PHOTIC SNEEZE REFLEX: THE TENDENCY TO SNEEZE IN BRIGHT LIGHT.

SCIENTISTS THINK CERTAIN GENES MAY MAKE SOME DOGS ESPECIALLY FRIENDLY.

MOTION SICKNESS

According to scientists, a single gene doesn't influence whether you get motion sickness—at least 35 genes do! Motion sickness happens when your different senses send conflicting messages to your brain.

SLEEP

Scientists believe that DNA can influence how long and how well you sleep. They also think it might influence whether you tend to have nightmares and what time you naturally wake up.

Genes may influence whether you have MISOPHONIA—a DISLIKE of some COMMON SOUNDS, such as PEOPLE CHEWING!

MUSICAL TALENT

Having a hard time hitting the right notes? Researchers think that your genes might be throwing you off key. But don't worry—they also say that environment and practice make up a big part of musical talent!

FEAR

From fear of heights to fear of public speaking, scientists are learning that our genes can contribute to whether or not we dislike high-up places and more. This trait would have helped our ancestors steer clear of dangerous places where they could fall.

CAN I CLONE MYSELF?

Imagine: A version of you to take out the trash, another to do homework ... you could conquer the world with an army of YOU! That is, if cloning worked that way. Cloning is not a magical duplication machine as in science fiction. It's real, but it raises important questions about whether science can be harmful. Cloning is making a copy of a living thing—from a cell to a whole animal—so that the copy has the exact same DNA as the original. But the clone still might not look exactly the same, as the clone's genes might combine or turn on and off differently (see p. 89). And the clone will probably not have the same personality. Making a human clone could be harmful to the clone—both physically and psychologically. Because of this, scientists do not try to clone humans. But scientists are learning more about how to clone healthy human cells to help treat diseases.

SCIENTISTS are using CLONING to SAVE an ENDANGERED SPECIES: the BLACK-FOOTED FERRET.

Dolly the Sheep

In 1996, scientists in Scotland took a live cell from an adult sheep. They copied the cell's DNA and placed the DNA copy into an egg cell taken from another sheep. Egg cells, found in female mammals, are the cells that are able to grow into new babies under the right conditions (see p. 88). This egg cell, which now contained the DNA to create a new animal, was placed into a female sheep where it could grow into a lamb.

When the lamb was born, it wasn't the offspring of the sheep that gave birth to it, but a clone of the original adult sheep! This little lamb, named Dolly, shocked the world. No one had thought it was possible to make a clone from a single adult cell. Dolly's birth meant a lot for science, but it was a pretty unremarkable event for Dolly. She went on to live a normal sheep's life.

IN THE 1950S, A TADPOLE BECAME THE FIRST CLONED ANIMAL.

WHY aren't all TWINS IDENTICAL?

IDENTICAL TWINS HAVE DIFFERENT FINGERPRINTS.

Some twins are identical and look the same. Some twins are fraternal and look very different. What's the difference? It's important to understand how human reproduction—the act of creating a new human—works. In humans, most females have special cells called egg cells. Most males have special cells called sperm cells. When a sperm cell meets an egg cell, it fertilizes it. This means that the two cells have joined together. A fertilized egg cell, called a zygote, receives DNA from both the male and female parents. This zygote can eventually form a new human inside the female's body. Sometimes, sperm cells fertilize more than one egg cell at the same time. Each zygote will receive DNA from both parents. However, the DNA can combine and express itself in different ways (see p. 72). This means that the twins will be born at the same time but will have different sets of DNA and may look very different.

(see p. 72)

WHY do IDENTICAL TWINS have DIFFERENCES?

Identical twins have the exact same DNA. How? Sometimes, one fertilized egg—a zygote—splits into two. This means that there are now two zygotes with exactly the same DNA. The twins born from these zygotes with identical DNA are called identical twins. So are identical twins, well, identical? Not completely! Identical twins do share the same DNA, and likely look identical to most people. But they often also have slight differences, especially as they grow older. Many of these differences come from the twins' environments and the different lives they lead. Other differences might happen when certain genes turn off or on in each twin (see p. 76).

(see p. 76).

DOGS can tell IDENTICAL TWINS APART.

WHY don't many **PEOPLE** have **RED HAIR?**

Only about 2 percent of the world's population has genetically red hair. This is because the gene linked to red hair is a recessive gene. Genes can be either dominant or recessive. This means that some genes are "stronger" or "louder" than others. For example, brown-eye genes are dominant while blue-eye genes are recessive. If a child receives a blue-eye gene from one parent and a brown-eye gene from the other, the child will likely have brown eyes since that gene is dominant. Similarly, for a child to have the gene that's linked to red hair, her biological parents must also both carry this gene and pass it on. Blonde hair is recessive, too, so why is it more common than red hair? This is because the gene for red hair is also linked to other genes. That means that these genes all need to be present to create naturally red hair.

IRELAND HAS THE HIGHEST PERCENTAGE OF REDHEADS IN THE WORLD.

Naturally Rare

Humans aren't the only animals that can inherit rare genes. Get to know these genetically rare colorings of the animal kingdom.

Scientists think REDHEADS may be more likely to be LEFT-HANDED.

PIEBALD

One genetic variant can cause patches of skin and fur that lack pigment and appear totally white. This can lead to a black-and-white coloring or a coat with white spots.

ALBINISM

Like piebald coloring, animals with albinism have a gene variant that prevents the creation of pigment. However, animals with albinism lack pigment over their entire bodies.

CHIMERA

Animals with this rare genetic variant are known as chimeras. The variant causes the cells of some animals to contain more than one set of DNA. This can give animals a blend of different coat patterns.

WHAT DO MY
GENES TELL PEOPLE?

DNA influences so much that people who study it can learn a lot about you without ever seeing you in person. Scientists who study DNA are able to "read" your DNA to learn what genes you have, and which are most likely to express themselves. Here are some examples of what a scientist could learn.

WHAT YOU MIGHT LOOK LIKE

By reading your DNA, a scientist could identify more than just your hair and eye color. For example, they could also likely figure out if you have a cleft chin (a small dimple on a person's chin). They could even learn whether you have wet or dry earwax!

WHERE YOU'RE FROM

By comparing your DNA to databases of DNA from history and from populations around the world, scientists would be able to figure out the most likely places that your ancestors lived.

WHO YOU'RE RELATED TO

Similarly, by searching for identical segments of DNA, scientists could find any relatives who had also let scientists study their DNA.

YOUR HEALTH

By looking at your genetic markers, scientists could tell you what health conditions you might develop later on in life.

CAN DNA TEACH US HISTORY?

Q: WHAT MADE YOU WANT TO BE A BIOLOGIST, AND HOW DID YOU GET STARTED ON THIS PARTICULAR STUDY?

A: As a child, I loved doing experiments, whether it was taking something apart or building something from scratch.

These days, the power of our DNA and genes fascinates me! Because St. Helena is so remote and has such a uniquely complex past, I was curious to investigate its history through the study of DNA.

Q: HOW DO YOU COLLECT AND STUDY DNA?

A: From the skeletal remains that were excavated from the burial ground, I carefully collected the bones that would be best for analyzing ancient DNA, including the petrous bones, teeth, and parts of the hand and foot bones. A person's DNA includes a range of information about everything from eye color to ancestral origins.

Q: WHAT ARE SOME THINGS YOU HAVE LEARNED—OR ARE HOPING TO LEARN—BY ANALYZING THE DNA?

A: Studying the DNA of this population can tell us so much about where they came from, what their lives were like, and even where their descendants live today. The main question I hope to answer is: What was the extent of liberation for these enslaved Africans?

Q: HOW WILL THIS INFORMATION DEEPEN OUR KNOWLEDGE OF HISTORY?

A: This study will provide the first ever data on the identities of this unique historical African population, allowing their ancestry to be traced back several generations and connecting them to modern populations around the world.

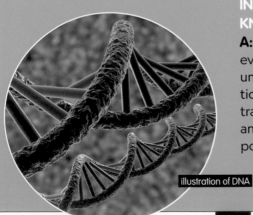

illustration of DNA

Gretchen Johnson is an American biologist. She studies the DNA found in the skeletons of formerly enslaved people from the mid-19th century who were liberated on the island of St. Helena, located in the South Atlantic Ocean some 1,600 miles (2,575 km) from the coast of Angola.

Here lie several
"**Liberated Africans**"
originally buried in
Rupert's Valley in the 1800s.
These people and others still buried in
Rupert's Valley were taken from their
homelands in Africa under the
Transatlantic slave trade.
...ed on slave vessels or in
... they were brought after
...by the British Royal Navy.
...finally rest in peace.

WHAT is my BRAIN MADE OF?

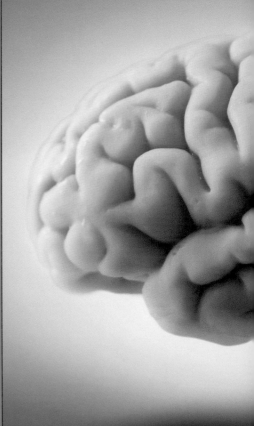

Your brain is one of your most important organs. It helps control motion, thought, memory, and much, much more. But what exactly is it? Your brain is a somewhat squishy mass of gray matter and white matter. Both types of matter are made largely of water and fat. Gray matter accounts for about 40 percent of your brain. It contains billions—about 100 billion to be exact—of special cells called neurons (see p. 102). White matter makes up the other 60 percent. This white matter is made up of extensions called dendrites that branch off from neurons. It also includes nerve fibers called axons that connect the neurons. All of this brain matter is soft—some scientists say it has the texture of Jell-O! And though it controls most of your functions, the brain matter itself cannot feel pain.

Get Brainy

Boost your brainpower and test your knowledge with this just-for-fun quiz on ... brains!

1. What is your brain?
a. a muscle
b. an organ
c. a sense

2. True or False:
Humans have the largest brains on the planet.

3. How much does the average human brain weigh?
a. three pounds (1.4 kg)
b. half a pound (0.2 kg)
c. 10 pounds (4.5 kg)

4. How many neurons are in the human brain?
a. 100
b. 10 million
c. 100 billion

5. True or False:
Your brain is made of fat.

With all the electricity it makes, your **BRAIN** could **POWER A LIGHTBULB.**

AN OCTOPUS HAS NINE BRAINS.

ANSWERS: 1. b; 2. false; 3. a; 4. c; 5. true

WHY is my BRAIN WRINKLY?

Scientists have long been interested in the folds found in human brains. Many researchers think these folds may even hold the secrets to what makes human beings so smart! Experts think that the wrinkles are the body's way of packing as much brain matter into your skull as possible. The brain's folds and whorls allow for more surface space on the brain. As your brain grows, instead of expanding outward, it folds in on itself and remains compact. The wrinkles might also allow us to think more quickly. Because the wrinkles are close together, this shortens the distance that messages need to travel from neuron to neuron. So how do the wrinkles form? Scientists aren't sure. Some experts think this might be because some parts of the brain grow faster than others. Others think that the neurons might pull toward each other, causing the tissue of the brain to fold and wrinkle.

SAY WHAT?!

ALBERT EINSTEIN'S BRAIN HAD MORE WRINKLES THAN MOST OTHER HUMANS' BRAINS.

The **WRINKLES** in the **BRAIN** are called **GYRI** and **SULCI.**

SAY WHAT?!

A GIANT SQUID'S BRAIN IS SHAPED LIKE A DOUGHNUT.

BRAIN ANATOMY

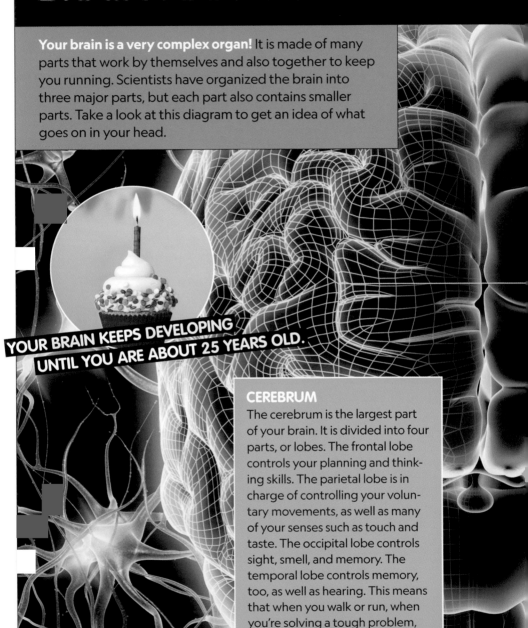

Your brain is a very complex organ! It is made of many parts that work by themselves and also together to keep you running. Scientists have organized the brain into three major parts, but each part also contains smaller parts. Take a look at this diagram to get an idea of what goes on in your head.

YOUR BRAIN KEEPS DEVELOPING UNTIL YOU ARE ABOUT 25 YEARS OLD.

CEREBRUM
The cerebrum is the largest part of your brain. It is divided into four parts, or lobes. The frontal lobe controls your planning and thinking skills. The parietal lobe is in charge of controlling your voluntary movements, as well as many of your senses such as touch and taste. The occipital lobe controls sight, smell, and memory. The temporal lobe controls memory, too, as well as hearing. This means that when you walk or run, when you're solving a tough problem, or when you're remembering your previous meal, your cerebrum is at work.

INFORMATION CAN TRAVEL THROUGH YOUR BRAIN AT 268 MILES AN HOUR (431.3 KM/H).

CEREBELLUM

If the cerebrum controls your major movements, the cerebellum fine-tunes them. The cerebellum allows you to balance and is in charge of your muscles. It also helps make certain movements you learn— such as riding a bike— become natural to you.

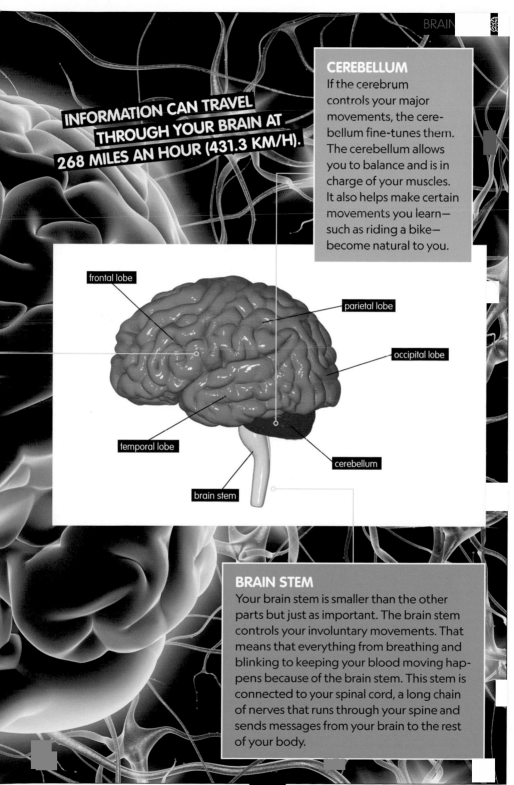

frontal lobe

parietal lobe

occipital lobe

temporal lobe

cerebellum

brain stem

BRAIN STEM

Your brain stem is smaller than the other parts but just as important. The brain stem controls your involuntary movements. That means that everything from breathing and blinking to keeping your blood moving happens because of the brain stem. This stem is connected to your spinal cord, a long chain of nerves that runs through your spine and sends messages from your brain to the rest of your body.

HOW does my BRAIN WORK?

Your brain helps you move, think, breathe, remember, feel, and much more. How does it do all of that? Your brain is made up of brain cells called neurons. Nerve fibers run between these neurons and also to the rest of your body. To function, your brain relies on receiving and sending messages. Small branching extensions on the neurons, known as dendrites, receive these signals and pass them to the neurons. Your neurons then interpret these signals to understand what is happening in your body. The neurons also send signals back out to instruct your body what to do, such as how to squeeze a ball, write a word, or digest your food. It sends these signals along your nerves. Your brain uses these messages to help control your body and its functions, such as breathing or the jobs your organs do. The three major parts of your brain—the cerebrum, cerebellum, and brain stem—work to control different functions (see p. 100).

One scientist thinks that, based on the SIZE of its BRAIN, *Tyrannosaurus rex* would have been about AS SMART AS A CHIMPANZEE.

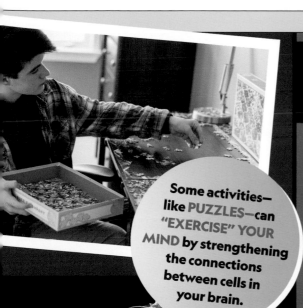

Some activities—like PUZZLES—can "EXERCISE" YOUR MIND by strengthening the connections between cells in your brain.

Biggest Brains

BIG ...

3.5 pounds
(1.6 kg)

BOTTLENOSE DOLPHIN

BIGGER ...

10.6 pounds
(4.8 kg)

ELEPHANT

BIGGEST!

20 pounds
(9 kg)

SPERM WHALE

WHY do I SOUND like ME?

Quick—what body part controls your voice? If you said your vocal cords, you're not wrong. These are folds inside your larynx, the tube that forms an air passage to your lungs. When you breathe out air to speak, the vocal cords rub together and vibrate, creating sound. You then use your mouth to shape the sound. But the real puppet master is your brain. Your brain controls these parts to help you talk. It also translates your thoughts into words. Your brain forms ideas, prepares them for speech, and then passes this information to another part of your brain that controls your mouth's movements. Once you speak, many things influence what your voice sounds like. This includes hormones, the way you move your mouth, how you breathe, your environment, and your genes. And what else? Your brain! Scientists have learned that your brain influences the rhythm in which you speak as well as the pitch.

GREAT SAC-WINGED BAT MOMS SPEAK "BABY TALK" TO THEIR PUPS.

SAY WHAT?!

SAY WHAT?!

A NUMBER OF ANIMALS, FROM ELEPHANTS TO ORCAS, HAVE BEEN RECORDED TRYING TO COPY HUMAN SPEECH.

Humans often use wordless sounds—like **WHOOPS** or **HOLLERS**—to express emotions such as **EXCITEMENT** or **HAPPINESS.**

WHY do I feel EMOTIONS?

Your emotions are influenced by something called the limbic system. This is a collection of small areas right under your cerebrum. These parts of the brain react to things around you by sending messages to your body. Scientists think that these emotions allow you to react quickly to different types of situations. For example, anger can help animals in the same way that fear does. When the brain encounters a difficult situation a person can't avoid, it may react by increasing aggression—in other words, making a person feel angry. For our ancestors, this response could help them defend themselves or appear scary to get out of tight spots. Similarly, when people encounter good situations, the brain often releases certain chemicals that make them feel happy. This could have led our ancestors to seek out safe situations. However, emotions may also have developed to serve a social purpose. Emotions let animals bond and work together, making a community stronger.

DOGS can SMELL different EMOTIONS.

WHY do 😱 I get SCARED?

Getting scared can be no fun. But for as long as life has been on Earth, animals have relied on fear to help them survive. Fear is the body's natural response to situations that may be dangerous. When a person sees something that might be threatening, a small area deep within their brain starts to act. This section is called the amygdala. It alerts the rest of your body to be prepared to either run away or defend itself. Called the "fight or flight response," this often results in a faster heartbeat, sweaty palms, heavy breathing, and more.

But why do situations that are pretty safe—such as riding a roller coaster or speaking in public—cause fear? This is because your brain can still see these things as threats. Your brain might react to the height and speed of a fast ride or the huge crowd of people before you.

FEAR may also be linked to a feel-good hormone called DOPAMINE—which is why many people like roller coasters.

WHY do I BREATHE automatically?

You are constantly moving, even when you think you're staying still. This is because your body is always performing involuntary actions: the actions that your body naturally takes without having to think about it. So if you're not controlling these movements, what is? The answer is your brain. Your brain controls something called the autonomic nervous system. This system manages breathing, your internal organs, sweat, and saliva. Your brain oversees this system by sending and receiving messages to and from the rest of your body. Your brain constantly gets information about how much oxygen and carbon dioxide are in your blood. It reacts to this by sending messages to your respiratory system to bring in air and then relax to let the air out (see p. 28). (see p. 28) Similarly, your brain monitors other things, such as how dry your eyes are or how much saliva is currently in your mouth. Then it sends signals to your body to blink or swallow.

HORSES CAN BREATHE ONLY THROUGH THEIR NOSE (NOT THROUGH THEIR MOUTH).

SAY WHAT?!

WHAT?!
SAY

SCIENTISTS THINK THAT YOUR FINGERS AND TOES WRINKLE IN WATER AS PART OF AN AUTONOMIC FUNCTION TO HELP YOU GRIP THINGS WHEN YOU'RE WET.

On average, **PEOPLE BREATHE IN** and **OUT** around **20,000 times** each day.

WHY do I SLEEP?

Is sleep really necessary? You bet! In fact, animals need sleep to survive. But sleep is still somewhat of a mystery to scientists. Different animals sleep different amounts of time. Animals' brains also function differently from those of other animals during sleep. On top of that, most animals are vulnerable to predators when they sleep. Despite these odd contradictions, scientists have figured out a few key things that happen during sleep. You might be asleep, but your brain is not! In humans, the body and brain both heal themselves and regain energy. The brain also stores information and turns it into memories. It gets rid of waste while you sleep. But what causes sleep in the first place? The brain. When it is time for you to sleep—for many mammals, that usually means when it gets dark—your brain releases a sleep hormone called melatonin. This hormone makes you feel drowsy. Your brain also tells your muscles to relax. And once it's lights out for you, your brain can get to work!

Some people dream in BLACK and WHITE (rather than in COLOR).

Day or Night

Many mammals, such as humans, sleep during the night. This allows mammals to stay warm during the day, hunt, and see easily. But many animals are nocturnal, meaning they're awake at night and asleep during the day. Check out these reasons why.

TEMPERATURE
Some animals in hot places such as deserts sleep during the day to beat the heat.

SAFETY
For some animals, coming out at night is safer because there aren't as many predators around.

DINNER
For other animals, coming out at night means they can hunt other nocturnal animals.

GIRAFFES CAN SLEEP STANDING UP.

WHY can't I HEAR myself THINK?

When you think, can you hear a voice in your head? Do you practice speeches in your mind? Do you sometimes have unspoken conversations with yourself that only you can hear? This is totally normal, and it's called an internal monologue. Scientists aren't sure where a person's internal monologue comes from. Since the brain controls how thoughts develop, most believe that the brain also influences your inner voice. But the rest is still a bit of a mystery. Some experts have theorized that the internal voice is the brain's way of drowning out other sounds to help you think. Another theory is that your brain uses this internal voice to help you hear other sounds when you speak. This could help you tell the difference between your voice and the sounds around you so that you can still hear what's going on while you talk.

SAY WHAT?!

SOME PEOPLE WHO ARE DEAF HAVE SAID THAT THEIR INTERNAL MONOLOGUE CONSISTS OF IMAGES AND SIGN LANGUAGE.

SAY WHAT?!

SCIENTISTS KNOW THAT DOGS THINK BUT DON'T KNOW IF DOGS ALSO HAVE A VERSION OF AN INTERNAL MONOLOGUE.

Can't hear an **INTERNAL VOICE?** You're not alone! Many people **DO NOT USE an** INTERNAL MONOLOGUE TO THINK.

WHY can't I REMEMBER EVERYTHING?

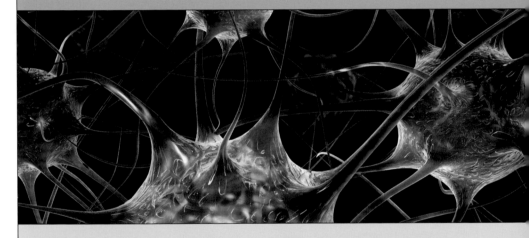

Quick—what did you eat for lunch two Mondays ago? Most likely, you can't remember. But you probably do remember celebrating your last birthday, seeing your favorite movie for the first time, or your last vacation. There's a scientific reason why we can remember some things but not others. At its most basic, a memory is stored information. But let's take a closer look. When your brain is active, your neurons are sending electric signals to each other and to your body (see p. 102). The ability to recall the paths that those neurons took at a given time is a memory. Sometimes, such as when you are feeling strong emotions or experiencing something you've never done before, the path is much stronger and easier to retrace. But during a routine action like eating lunch, the path that those neurons took may be faint and harder for you to recall.

Scientists think DOLPHINS have the LONGEST MEMORIES of all nonhuman animals.

WHY can't I REMEMBER BEING LITTLE?

Even though memories are just the pathways made between our neurons, most people don't have many—if any—memories before the age of about four years old. Scientists aren't sure why. Some experts say there is a difference between the ability to remember things that recently happened and those that happened a while ago. This is called short-term memory and long-term memory. Short-term memory is often used for items that need to be recalled soon, such as where you parked your bike. However, these memories are only temporary. It may be that babies are much better at using short-term than long-term memory until their brains have grown more. But some scientists say that the reason we often don't remember our early years may be because our brains grow quickly. A child's brain grows so quickly that as the new matter forms, it may break up old pathways—and memories.

Goldfish can REMEMBER THINGS for SIX MONTHS.

WHY do I get ANGRY when I'm HUNGRY?

It's almost lunchtime, and you're hungry—not only that, you feel super irritated! To understand why, let's first look at what causes hunger in the body. Your body needs food to make energy. When blood sugar and insulin levels in your body start to get low, your body uses a special hormone, called ghrelin, to alert your brain. Your brain then produces special molecules that cause you to feel hungry. (A very similar process happens when your stomach is full.) But what about that "hangry" feeling? When your body is low on energy, that means it's also low on the sugars and other materials that help keep your emotions in check. However, scientists think being "hangry" may prove useful for animals. An animal that starts to feel more aggression when it gets hungry might have a better chance of snagging a meal. All the same—better to grab a snack!

HUMMINGBIRDS NEED TO FEED ON NECTAR EVERY 10 TO 15 MINUTES.

SAY WHAT?!

SAY **WHAT?!**

IT CAN TAKE AN ANACONDA WEEKS TO DIGEST A LARGE MEAL.

LACK of SLEEP can make PEOPLE feel HUNGRIER.

WHY can't I READ MINDS?

Many people would love to have brain superpowers, such as the ability to read minds (called telepathy) or the ability to move objects with your mind (called telekinesis). For telekinesis to work in real life, our brains would have to be able to directly influence physical matter. And for telepathy to work, our brains would have to be able to send messages not just within our own bodies but also to other brains. Currently, the human body doesn't have any way to do this. But that doesn't mean it's entirely impossible ... in fact, some scientists say that we already can read minds! According to researchers, the ability to tell what someone is thinking based on their facial expression alone is a form of mind reading. Scientists are also developing technology that reads and translates our brain activity. This could potentially let us speak or interact with the world—without moving or saying a word!

Some companies are trying to develop MACHINES that can READ THOUGHTS based on a BRAIN'S ELECTRICAL ACTIVITY.

Body Myths Busted

Get ready to bust some myths about the human body!

MYTH! WE USE ONLY 10 PERCENT OF OUR BRAINS.

This popular myth claims that most people don't use up to 90 percent of their brains. But it's not true! Brain scans show that humans are using most of their brains almost all the time.

MYTH! YOUR GENES CONTROL WHETHER YOU CAN CURL YOUR TONGUE.

If you can't curl your tongue, don't blame your biological parents! Studies showed that even in cases of identical siblings who share the same DNA, some can roll their tongue and some can't.

MYTH! YOU LOSE THE MOST HEAT THROUGH YOUR HEAD.

While it's a smart idea to wear a hat in cold weather, your head still makes up only about 10 percent of your body. The amount of heat you lose through your head is proportional to that.

ANTS COMMUNICATE THROUGH A TYPE OF CHEMICAL CALLED A PHEROMONE.

WHY do I DAYDREAM?

One minute you're sitting on a long bus ride, counting the minutes—the next, you're starring in a high-flying circus act! Daydreaming—the state of having your mind wander or imagining different scenarios—is totally normal. Researchers have long known that daydreaming is a way for people to relax during times of stress. But scientists have learned that it also helps you solve problems. Daydreaming allows people to imagine themselves in risky situations without experiencing any real risk. And just as important, your brain is highly active when you daydream. While you are daydreaming, your brain is problem-solving. You might not realize it, but your brain is likely working out things that might be bothering you. In fact, researchers in one study recommend taking a break if you're faced with a difficult problem. Taking time to work on something simpler or relax and daydream could help you figure things out. So dream away!

According to scientists, DAYDREAMING makes PEOPLE more CREATIVE.

WHY do I have NIGHTMARES?

When you sleep, your brain is still wide awake (see p. 110). The periods of sleep when your brain is most active are known as rapid eye movement sleep (REM sleep). Scientists believe that during REM sleep, activity in your cerebrum (see p. 100) causes you to hallucinate—or dream. Scientists aren't sure why this is, but they have theories. Many experts believe that dreaming might help you sort through and store your memories. It might also help you work through the things going on in your life or events from the past that you still think about. However, dreams can sometimes be downright scary. Again, scientists aren't sure why, but they think these could be reflections of stress or worries we have when we're awake. Scientists say that relaxing before bed and having a regular sleep schedule can help keep the nightmares away.

DOGS likely DREAM about their OWNERS.

WHY do I SEE STARS?

It's not quite like when a cartoon character gets bonked on the head and sees star shapes above them. But bright flashes or specks of light in your vision can occur in real life, too. (There's even a name for this phenomenon: photopsia.) Some causes are physical. If you rub your eyes, for example, tiny fibers can create the illusion of stars by rubbing or pulling the retina, a layer at the back of your eye. This can also happen when you sneeze. A whack on the head can cause brain cells to send out random signals. The brain then might interpret these as flashes of light. Other times, low blood pressure (sometimes caused by standing up too quickly) can cause the cells to signal in a similar way. In general, seeing stars is a natural reaction and nothing to worry about (though if you get hit hard on the head, you should have a doctor check it out).

BIRDS OFTEN SLEEP WITH ONE EYE OPEN.

SAY WHAT?!

SAY WHAT?!

BOX JELLYFISH HAVE FOUR TYPES OF EYES AND 24 EYES TOTAL.

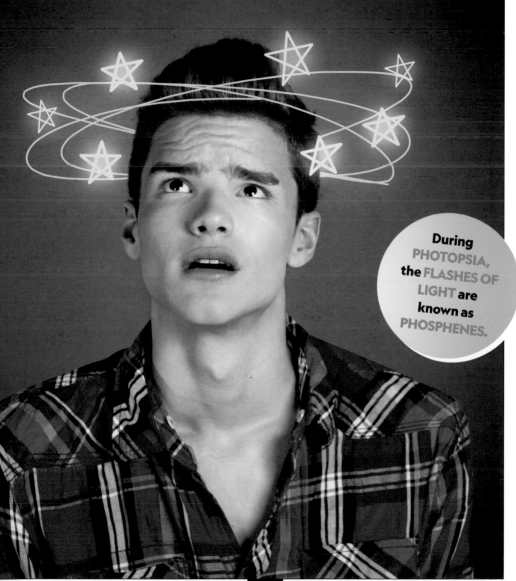

During **PHOTOPSIA,** the **FLASHES OF LIGHT** are known as **PHOSPHENES.**

CAN SCIENTISTS ALTER MEMORIES?

Q&A WITH STEVE RAMIREZ

Q: WHAT MADE YOU WANT TO STUDY THE BRAIN AND MEMORY?

A: Memories are like a time machine. We can travel back to the past and revisit any moment we want. I wanted to know how this time machine worked and if we could also build new time machines of memory in the brain.

Q: WHAT ARE SOME OF THE EXPERIMENTS YOU DO TO STUDY BRAINS?

A: We find where memories in the brain are located and turn those memories on or off. We also take some of the corners where memories live in the brain and then put them under a microscope to see what they physically look like!

Q: HOW COULD ALTERING MEMORIES HELP PEOPLE?

A: Altering memories could help us better remember some of the most positive moments of our lives, while also weakening some of our more negative memories. Our goal is to make memory something that strengthens our brains and ourselves.

Q: WHAT ARE SOME SURPRISING THINGS YOU HAVE LEARNED ABOUT HUMAN BRAINS?

A: Memories are not like videos of the past but in fact are warped each time we recall them! It's like we're applying a filter to a memory every time we recall it, and so the memory ends up being slightly different every time.

BONUS!

Steve's Tips for Improving Memory

A lot of what we can do to improve memory includes exercising regularly, getting a good night's sleep, eating a healthy diet, and staying connected socially with friends and family!

Steve Ramirez is an American neuroscientist, a type of scientist who analyzes the brain. He is studying how to purposely tinker with memories—including how to help people forget, help them remember, or even implant new memories that never really happened.

WHY do I have SNOT?

Ugh—snot, boogers, mucus! Why do we even have any of it? Because it's really important! To get air to your lungs, you breathe in—usually through your nose. But sometimes you inhale tiny particles of dust, pollen, dirt, or bacteria that are in the air. To protect your lungs, your nose is coated in a sticky substance called mucus. This mucus is created by small organs called glands that line your nose and throat. Mucus—along with your nose hairs—catches and traps any foreign objects that you inhale. This causes boogers. While snot and boogers are normally mostly clear, you might have noticed that when you're fighting off a cold your snot turns greenish or yellow. This color comes from your white blood cells. When you have a cold, white blood cells rush to defend your body. After these cells die, they enter into your snot, turning it that green-yellow color.

ECHIDNAS sometimes BLOW SNOT BUBBLES to CLEAR their NOSE of dirt.

Survival of the Slimiest

PARROTFISH SLEEP IN MUCUS COCOONS TO KEEP AWAY PARASITES.

Humans aren't the only animals to produce their own slime. Hagfish are eel-shaped ocean animals that feed on the dead bodies of other ocean creatures. To defend themselves against predators, they have a special trick: They slime them! Hagfish use special glands to send out proteins that, when they mix with seawater, turn into a sticky slime that slows down predators. This slime—though it seems icky—could also be really important for humans. Because the slime is both flexible and super strong, scientists are searching for a way to make it into an environmentally friendly material that can be used for everything from clothing to ropes. Hagfish slime sneakers? Sign us up!

WHY do
I like getting
GROSSED
OUT?

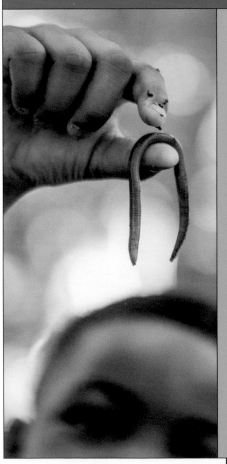

Being grossed out is a natural feeling. In fact, it probably helped your human ancestors stay safe (see p. 56). Even so, many people love to read about or investigate icky things. That's perfectly natural, too! Scientists think people may be drawn to disgust because we seek out safe versions of things that are dangerous. Learning about gross things in a safe way can cause a thrill in our brains. Some scientists even think that safely getting grossed out might prepare us in case we ever need to know what to do in future scenarios. Other scientists think that it might have something to do with our natural curiosity ... and our need to eat. When our ancestors searched for food, they would have encountered a variety of options. Even if something smelled gross, it might also be good to eat. Your gusto for gross might stem from our ancestors' need to investigate it all!

SAY **WHAT?!**

SOME PEOPLE COLLECT TOENAIL CLIPPINGS.

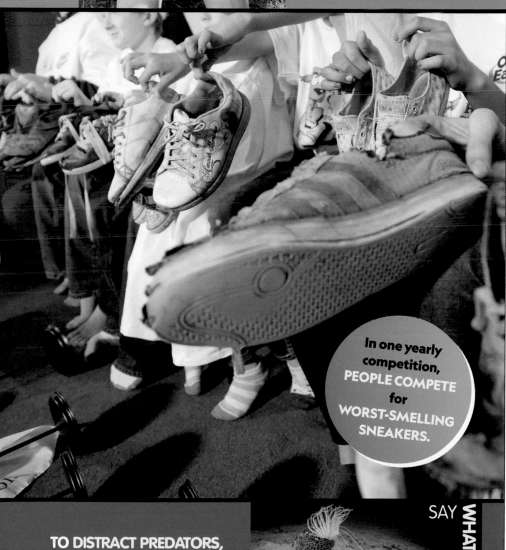

In one yearly competition, **PEOPLE COMPETE** for **WORST-SMELLING SNEAKERS.**

TO DISTRACT PREDATORS, SOME SEA CUCUMBERS POOP OUT THEIR OWN GUTS.

SAY **WHAT?!**

WHY do I get EYE BOOGERS?

Mucus lives in your nose (see p. 126), and it's also in your eyes! A thin covering over your eye produces mucus. This covering, called the conjunctiva, is responsible for keeping your eyes moist and safe. Any dust that enters your eye comes into contact with the conjunctiva and its mucus. When you blink, all that dust and mucus—plus any dead cells or skin oils—collects in the corners of your eyes. These sticky eye boogers have an official name: rheum. So why are there more after you sleep? And why are they crustier in the morning? That's because you aren't removing the rheum as you sleep, so it builds up over time. It also dries out, forming a crust—and sometimes even makes your eyelashes stick together.

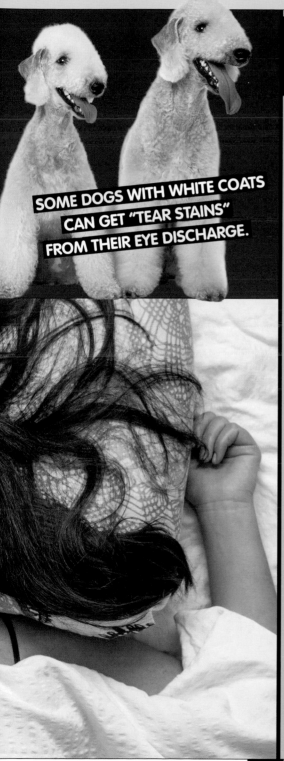

SOME DOGS WITH WHITE COATS CAN GET "TEAR STAINS" FROM THEIR EYE DISCHARGE.

Body Behavior

Match the gross body behavior to the correct animal below!

A When threatened, this animal uses small blood vessels around its eyes to shoot blood at would-be attackers.

B If this animal comes across a potential predator, it vomits a foul-smelling liquid.

C To mark its territory, this animal spins its tail to spray poop as far as it can.

EURASIAN ROLLER BIRD

SHORT-HORNED LIZARD

HIPPOPOTAMUS

131

WHY do I have DROOL?

Saliva, or spit, is a substance made by tiny organs in your mouth called salivary glands. Spit is made of water and chemicals and has several important jobs. The chemicals in your spit help break down food, beginning the digestion process before you've even swallowed (see p. 108). Your spit also coats the food you eat, making it easier to swallow. It coats your tongue, too, which helps keep your tongue moist, thus allowing you to taste the food. And your spit helps keep your mouth clean by clearing it of food particles and bacteria. So what causes drool? A person's mouth tends to water when they see or think about delicious food. This is because your brain sends a signal to your salivary glands. Other times, such as when you're asleep, you might drool. This can happen if your muscles are extra relaxed or if you aren't swallowing as much.

WHY can't I SPIT like a LLAMA?

Ptooey! **Llamas and alpacas can spit up to 10 feet (3 m) away.** How come people can't spit that far? Well, some people can! When you spit, you use your tongue to gather saliva that has collected in your mouth. You then use the muscles in your cheeks and lips to forcefully blow out the spit. Some people know how to use their face muscles to get extra distance on their spit. Others get their head and neck into the motion, and they even know how to use math to spit at the best angle for distance. In fact, the world record for spitting a cherry pit is more than 100 feet (30.5 m)! But people still can't spit quite like a llama does. That's because the llama isn't using spit! When llamas and alpacas spit to show that they are upset, they are often regurgitating the bile in their stomachs.

A CHAMELEON'S TONGUE is COATED in a MUCUS 400 times THICKER than HUMAN SALIVA.

GROSSEST ANIMALS

Snot, poop, drool—the human body can be gross. But so can the rest of the animal kingdom! Check out this gallery of grossness.

PUPPIES OFTEN EAT FOOD THAT THEIR PARENTS THROW UP.

MESSIEST MUNCHER

Adult koalas survive by eating euca-lyptus. Koala babies, called joeys, eat their mom's poop! This special poop, called pap, helps joeys get nutrients.

SMELLIEST

The striped polecat, a small mammal found throughout much of Africa, protects itself by spray-ing a stinky liquid from glands near its rear end. This liquid is so foul-smelling that it makes even lions think twice.

WORST MANNERS

The skua seabird has a gross diet and manners to match. This bird bully will harass other birds until they vomit up their fishy meals ... which the skua will then gobble down! And if there's no vomit in sight? They sometimes turn to eating rotten meat.

MESSIEST HOMES

You might think your room is messy, but at least it isn't made with spit! Swiftlet birds build their nests out of sticks, twigs, bark ... and their own spit.

SLIMIEST

Velvet worms shoot out ropes of quick-hardening slime to capture their prey. With its meal immobilized, the worm then uses its own saliva to liquefy its prey's innards and suck them out.

VULTURES HAVE A SPECIAL ACID IN THEIR STOMACH THAT KEEPS THEM FROM GETTING SICK WHEN THEY EAT ROTTEN MEAT.

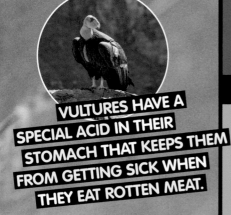

135

WHAT causes PIMPLES?

Almost everyone gets pimples at some point. Gross? Nope. Natural? Yes! But they can definitely be annoying, and even a little bit painful sometimes. Pimples are caused by blockages that happen in your skin. Your skin is covered with tiny openings called pores that let out sweat and natural oils. Your body often creates an oil called sebum to moisturize your skin. Sometimes, pores can get blocked by dirt, dead skin, or even too much sebum. This tends to trap the oil inside your pores. Trapped sebum can mix with the air and turn black in color, creating small dots called blackheads. If the pore closes up around the sebum, it stays white, creating whiteheads. Sometimes, trapped sebum or trapped bacteria can irritate the skin and cause a small red bump—a pimple.

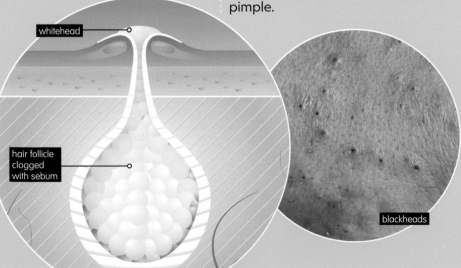

whitehead

hair follicle clogged with sebum

blackheads

SAY **WHAT?!**

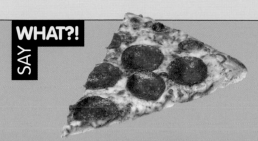

SCIENTISTS THINK IT'S A MYTH THAT CERTAIN FOODS LIKE PIZZA OR CHOCOLATE CAN CAUSE PIMPLES.

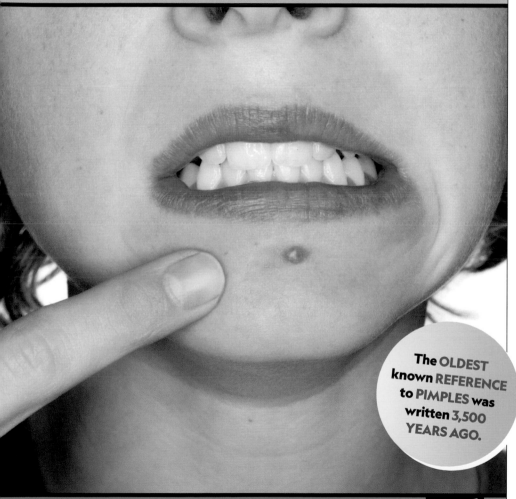

The OLDEST known REFERENCE to PIMPLES was written 3,500 YEARS AGO.

SAY **WHAT?!**

CATS AND DOGS CAN GET PIMPLES.

WHY do people PICK their NOSE?

Even though they might not admit to it, almost everyone picks their nose from time to time. The most common reason is to remove something uncomfortable from a nostril. Mucus, which lines our nostrils, helps trap foreign objects such as dust, bacteria, dirt, and dead skin cells. Our nose hairs work to block these items as well. Sometimes the mucus can harden into uncomfortable pieces that poke into our skin. Other times, accumulated mucus makes it harder to breathe or causes a stuffed-up feeling. Sometimes, people pick their nose out of boredom, or just because it feels good! So if everyone is doing it, why is it considered impolite? Well, boogers often contain dirt and germs, which can spread from your hands to someone else's!

Feeling Picky

Do animals pick their noses, too? You bet!

APES AND MONKEYS

Not only do apes and monkeys pick their noses, they use tools to do it. Scientists have recorded different kinds of monkeys and apes using sticks to dislodge boogers.

GIRAFFES

No hands? No problem! Giraffes use their long tongues to clean snot from their noses. They also use their tongues to clean their eyes and even their ears.

SEA LIONS

To clear blocked nasal passages, sea lions sneeze and even spit their mucus.

DOGS

Many animals, such as dogs and horses, let snot drip down their faces. Then they lick it up!

Scientists have discovered TINY OCEAN CREATURES that BUILD HUGE HOMES from their SNOT.

THE SAFEST WAY TO REMOVE BOOGERS IS BY GENTLY BLOWING YOUR NOSE INTO A TISSUE.

WHAT are SCABS and PUS?

If you've ever scraped your knee, you've probably gotten a scab. But what exactly is this crusty cover? When you scrape yourself, platelets—small pieces of cells in your blood—go to work. Platelets group together to form a barrier, or clot, that prevents blood from getting out. Eventually, the clot begins to dry out and harden into a scab. Scabs protect you by keeping germs and dirt out of your healing cut. So what about pus? It may look gross, but it's also there to help you. White blood cells in your body work to fight off infections. When the white blood cells die, they group together and form what you see as pus. Small amounts of pus are normally fine, but larger amounts can point to an infection.

SAY WHAT?!

BRUISES ARE CAUSED WHEN SMALL BLOOD VESSELS NEAR THE SKIN'S SURFACE GET DAMAGED.

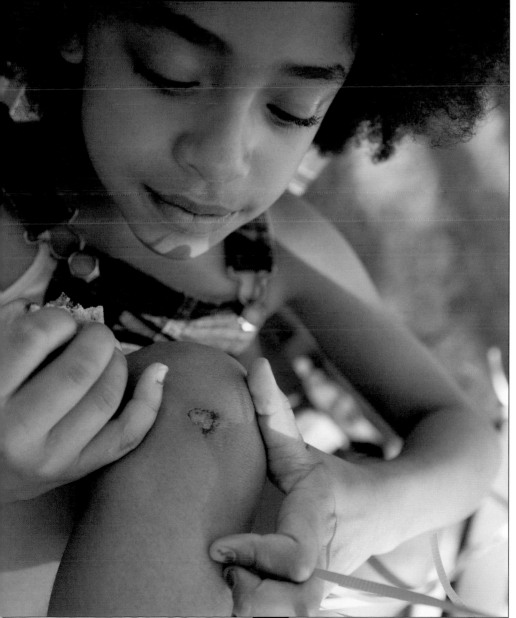

A PROTEIN IN DOG SALIVA CAN HELP HEAL THEIR WOUNDS.

WHY do POOPS look DIFFERENT?

SHARK POOP is GREEN.

After you eat, your digestive system collects the nutrients from your meal. The rest, along with dead cells and other waste, comes out as poop (see p. 26). Poop, or feces, is mostly made of water. It also contains those dead cells (often dead blood cells) and food remnants, as well as bacteria and bile (digestive juices) from your stomach. Your waste can look very different depending on what you've eaten and the state of your health. Because of the dead blood cells, most poop looks brown. Bile can also add a green shade. Different health conditions or foods can make poop look white, reddish, black, or yellow. Food and health also change what shape and firmness your waste has. Your body and diet can even impact how often you go. According to doctors, a healthy person should ideally poop once to twice a day and produce a somewhat firm log that sticks together.

WHY does PEE change COLORS?

Your urinary system, separate from your digestive system, focuses on getting rid of waste, or toxins, in your system. Two organs called kidneys do this by filtering your blood. After they have passed the good stuff—like water and nutrients—to your bloodstream, they send the rest to your bladder as urine. Urine is made up of water and waste products your body doesn't need. After it collects in your bladder, your brain signals to you that you need to pee. Most urine has a yellow color because of something called urochrome, which is a type of waste left over by your body. If you drink lots of water, there will be more water than urochrome present, so your urine will look clearer. But colorful foods—natural or dyed—as well as health conditions can change the color of your urine as well.

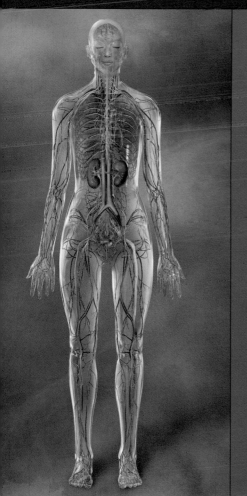

A WOMBAT'S POOP is CUBE-SHAPED.

WHAT's in a TOOT?

Whether you call it a toot, a fart, or passing gas, everyone does it! When you eat, you take in air as well as food. Your digestive system also creates other kinds of gas when it breaks down food. All this gas has to go somewhere ... so it comes out of your rear end! A lot of the time, your toot contains gases that don't smell. But sometimes, your stomach also makes a gas called hydrogen sulfide. This gas tends to smell like rotten eggs, and it's the reason some toots stink. Foods that have a lot of sulfur, a type of chemical, can make toots smell worse, too. Foods that are hard to digest can also cause you to toot more. For many people, this includes dairy foods. Beans, which are high in fiber, are also famous for causing toots.

SCIENTISTS THINK DINOSAURS MAY HAVE PASSED SO MUCH GAS THAT IT MADE EARTH WARMER.

ONE TYPE OF INSECT STUNS ITS PREY BY TOOTING ON IT.

beaded lacewing

Tooting Animals

Not all animals toot! In fact, scientists have begun to keep a database of which animals pass gas and which don't. So who hasn't ever dealt it? Many sea creatures don't pass gas. Birds also don't toot. Unlike humans, birds' stomachs don't have the type of bacteria that break down food and cause gas. Most mammals do toot—but not sloths! Because sloths digest so slowly, they are able to absorb the gas into their bloodstreams. They then breathe it out of their lungs.

For animals that do pass gas, tooting is pretty important. In fact, for manatees, it's necessary. Manatees have a special pouch that stores their gas. This gas helps them float in the water. When they want to dive deeper, they toot!

WHOOPEE CUSHION

WHY do I get BAD BREATH?

The human body is full of bacteria. Most of this bacteria is good for us, as it helps us break down food and helps fight off things that make us sick. We also have bacteria in our mouths. When we eat, this bacteria breaks down the food left over on our teeth and gums. But in the process, the bacteria also create chemicals that can stink. These chemicals are the source of most bad breath. They are also why our breath tends to smell worse in the morning: We've gone so long without brushing our teeth, eating, or drinking that the bacteria have had lots of time to create stinky smells. But sometimes, the food we eat is the culprit. Foods like garlic and onions can cause bad breath because they contain smelly oils that tend to stick around.

ACCORDING TO SCIENTISTS, WHALE BREATH SMELLS LIKE TOOTS AND ROTTEN FISH.

SAY WHAT?!

SAY WHAT?!

CERTAIN GASES IN YOUR STOMACH CAN MAKE YOUR BURPS SMELL LIKE ROTTEN EGGS.

It can be **HARD** for **PEOPLE** to **SMELL THEIR OWN BREATH** because we get **USED TO THINGS** we smell a lot.

WHAT is DANDRUFF?

Are those snowflakes on your head? Nope! That's dandruff. Dandruff is an extremely common occurrence that affects people's scalps. The scalp, or the top of the head, is covered in skin just like any other part of the body. Sometimes, scalp skin can flake off in tiny white patches, called dandruff. Dandruff isn't painful, but it can be itchy and annoying. What causes dandruff? Some scientists say that dandruff often happens when the scalp gets either too dry or too oily. However, other scientists say that a dry, flaky scalp is different from dandruff. But scientists agree that dandruff can be caused by an allergy, a medical condition, or a fungus.

SOME ANIMALS THAT SHED THEIR SKIN—SUCH AS GECKOS— EAT IT AFTERWARD.

Digging for Dandruff

Are humans the only animals that get dandruff? No way! All kinds of members of the animal kingdom get versions of flaky skin. In pets such as dogs, cats, rodents, and birds, this is known as pet dander. It is not harmful to the pet, but it can be itchy just like human dandruff. It can also cause allergies in people.

Reptiles don't usually get dandruff in quite the same way. Instead, they shed their old skin in one large piece. Well, most do! Archaeologists uncovered the fossil of a 125-million-year-old winged dinosaur called *Microraptor*—and its fossilized dandruff! This led scientists to discover that, unlike most modern-day reptiles, dinosaurs seem to have shed their skin in tiny pieces of dandruff.

About **HALF** of all **ADULTS** get **DANDRUFF.**

WHY does POOP SMELL?

Your body's waste contains food leftovers, dead blood cells, bile, and other stuff that's no longer needed. That combination may sound like enough of a big stink, but the main source of the smelliness comes from the bacteria in your stomach. When these bacteria break down food, they create gases and other stinky by-products. Part of the reason we tend to be disgusted by the smell of poop is because if we come into contact with it, that same bacteria can make us sick. Tiny molecules traveling through the air contact special cells in your nose called olfactory receptors (see p. 56). These receptors send messages to your brain, which interprets the messages as scents. The bad smell is a warning to stay away. If a person's poo smells extra stinky, it may be due to the foods they ate. The same foods that can make a toot stinky (see p. 144) can also make your waste extra ripe!

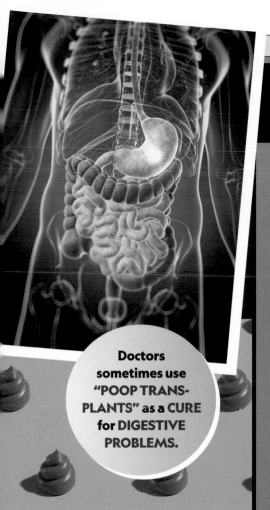

Fans of Feces

Human beings tend to naturally feel grossed out by poop. So why do some animals love it? Check out the reasons these animals are attracted to waste.

DOGS
Many scientists think that a dog's tendency to roll in poo may be a behavior left over from its wolf ancestors. By rolling in stinky things, wolves can mask their natural scents to better sneak up on prey.

DUNG BEETLES
Dung beetles often roll the waste from other animals into balls, and then steer these round pieces of poo to their young back home. There, they dine on the undigested pieces of food that remain in the waste.

AFRICAN DOUBLE-BANDED COURSER
One type of bird, the African double-banded courser, protects its egg by hiding it near antelope poop. Because the egg also resembles poop, hiding it near a pile of poop means that predators probably won't find it.

Doctors sometimes use "POOP TRANS-PLANTS" as a CURE for DIGESTIVE PROBLEMS.

WHY do I HAVE EARWAX?

Like many other sticky, "icky" things in your body, earwax is there to help you. Inside your ear, you have special tiny organs called glands. These glands create an oily substance called cerumen—or earwax. This waxy substance comes in two forms: wet or dry. Whether you have wet or dry earwax is determined by your genes. No matter its form, cerumen does several important things. Like other oils in your body, it helps keep your skin moist and prevent itchiness. It also helps fight bacteria. One way cerumen does this is through the special chemicals it contains that can fight off things that make us sick. Another way is by being so sticky! When foreign objects such as dirt and dust enter your ears, they get stuck—along with dead skin cells—in the earwax there.

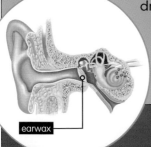

earwax

SOME CATS LIKE LICKING HUMAN EARWAX.

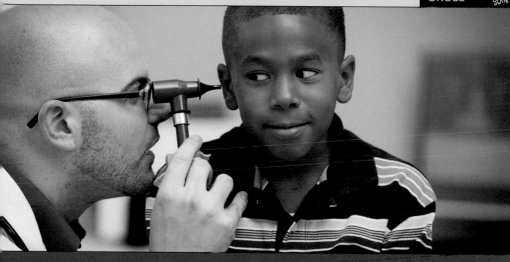

CAN I have TOO MUCH EARWAX?

Earwax might seem gross, but it's what keeps your ears clean. Most of the time, old earwax naturally comes out when you clean your ears. This can be done in the shower or with a damp cloth. However, earwax can build up in the ear and form a block in the ear canal. Sometimes, this can harden, making it difficult to remove. A blockage like this is called impacted earwax. Impacted earwax tends to happen more often to adults, who secrete more cerumen. It normally isn't dangerous, but buildups can be painful, make hearing harder, or cause a slight ringing sound called tinnitus. Luckily doctors have many safe ways of removing buildup. Some use small suction devices that pull the earwax from the canal. Others have a special tool, called a curette, that looks like a small spoon. They use this to scoop the wax from your ears. *Mmm, cerumen, anyone?*

You can **TELL HOW OLD** a **WHALE** is by looking at its **EARWAX.**

WHY do I THROW UP?

Throwing up is never pleasant, but it is important. Vomiting is your body's way of ejecting harmful foods or liquids. If you've eaten something that could make you sick, such as spoiled food, your body will try to get rid of it. First, your body sends a message to your brain that something isn't right. Your brain then tells your salivary glands (see p. 132) to start making spit, which will protect your teeth. Your stomach muscles also begin to squeeze, until the contents of your stomach are forced up and out. Sometimes, people who see vomit also feel the urge to puke. Scientists believe that this was a social response that developed over time. Humans who spent time together often ate the same things. If you see someone vomiting, your brain worries that you may have eaten something bad, too, and sends a signal for you to get rid of it.

SOME FROGS VOMIT UP THEIR ENTIRE STOMACH ... THEN PULL IT BACK IN.

SAY WHAT?!

SCIENTISTS CREATED A
VOMITING ROBOT TO STUDY
HOW ILLNESSES SPREAD.

HOW do scientists make new VACCINES?

Viruses are small particles that need hosts, such as animals, to survive. Viruses usually damage their hosts, making them sick. Luckily, scientists can develop vaccines. Vaccines teach your immune system how to fight certain viruses. By getting a vaccine, you can avoid catching the virus altogether or if you do catch it, you will probably get less sick. But viruses are always changing and growing, so scientists continually need to create new vaccines. In laboratories, scientists are able to safely study a new virus. They can change the genetic code of a particular virus so that it is very weak or cannot harm people. They can also remove part of the virus so that the virus can't replicate, or copy, itself. Vaccines containing this changed virus are given to people. The body learns to fight off the virus without much risk because the changed virus cannot fight back. Then if the body encounters the virus in the wild, it will already know what to do because it was "trained" by the vaccine to fight the weakened virus.

Inventing Vaccines

MOST SCIENTISTS DO NOT CONSIDER VIRUSES TO BE ALIVE.

Learning how to make vaccines wasn't easy for scientists. Humans around the world had a basic understanding that someone could be immune to an illness—meaning that they weren't able to catch it. But it wasn't until experiments done in the late 1700s that people began to understand exactly how immunity works, and how to harness that power to create vaccines. In 1796, a disease called smallpox was harming many people in England. A doctor and scientist named Edward Jenner had an idea. He took a small sample of a related—but less harmful—disease called cowpox and introduced it to a patient. The patient's body learned how to fight off cowpox—and, because it was so similar, smallpox as well. The patient was then immune to smallpox. It took many years for people to understand how to safely distribute vaccines widely, but Jenner took the first step.

The word "VACCINE" comes from the LATIN WORD for COW: VACCA.

WHAT would happen to me on MARS?

USING CURRENT SPACESHIP TECHNOLOGY, IT WOULD TAKE ABOUT SEVEN MONTHS TO TRAVEL TO MARS.

Scientists are working hard to make human travel to Mars possible. Some even think that eventually humans could build colonies there. But Mars is different from Earth—very different. How would life on the red planet impact the human body? The lack of gravity would likely affect our muscles, which are designed to work against Earth's strong gravity to hold us up and let us move (see p. 22). In weaker gravity, our muscles would not have to work as hard and would likely weaken over time. The spaces between our vertebrae would probably expand, making us taller. Mars also has a thin atmosphere, which means that human bodies would be vulnerable to radiation from the sun. On top of all that? Scientists think that the dust on Mars is toxic. Experts would have to solve this problem—as well as figure out how to provide oxygen, water, and food.

ASTRONAUTS use EXERCISE MACHINES in SPACE to keep their MUSCLES STRONG.

WHAT if
I LIVED on a
SPACE STATION?

OK, so living on Mars seems tough. But what about calling a space station or a spaceship home? Astronauts spend long periods of time on the International Space Station that orbits Earth, after all. In some respects, life on a space station would be easier than life on Mars; people can more easily regulate water and food. But scientists still need to solve many of the same issues that would affect you on Mars. Currently, we don't have the technology to simulate gravity on a spacecraft, so life on high results in weakened muscles and lengthened spines. You would also still be exposed to radiation without an atmosphere to protect you. And living in a small, cramped space station might cause stress for many people. But hey, at least there's no toxic Mars dust!

WILL people keep EVOLVING?

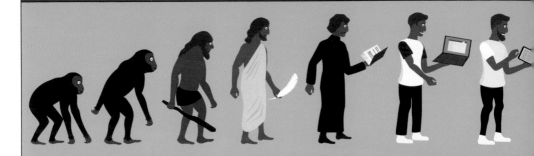

Not only are humans still evolving, but you can even see some of the more (relatively) recent changes. One example is an organ known as your appendix. Scientists aren't sure what it does. Some think that it might be a home for your healthy gut bacteria. Others think the organ is left over from our human ancestors and that we no longer need it. Our ancestors also used giant molars in the back of their mouths to grind food. Today, these are known as wisdom teeth, and many people are born without them. So what could future evolutions look like? Some scientists think we will continue to get taller and larger, as we have already been doing. Others think that because humans across the world travel and interact more, we may start to look more alike. But we also may develop in surprising ways. Studies have shown that some of the Bajau people of Southeast Asia, who typically hold their breath for a long time when diving underwater, have larger than average spleens. This organ can then store more oxygen, allowing them to dive longer without drawing a breath.

SCIENTISTS THINK THAT THE GINKGO BILOBA TREE EVOLVED BERRIES THAT SMELL LIKE ROTTEN MEAT TO ATTRACT DINOSAURS.

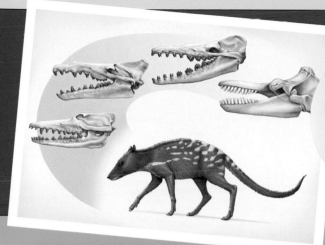

BEFORE they EVOLVED to live in the water, WHALE ANCESTORS WALKED on LAND.

Different Places, Different Changes

Scientists think that huge changes to our environments could also, over time, change the way humans look. Check out these hypothetical changes that scientists have imagined.

PLACE

PLACE

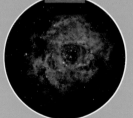

PLACE

An Earth where water covers even more of the planet

Earth during an Ice Age

Space

CHANGES

Webbed feet and hands for swimming and eyes like a cat's to see in dark water

CHANGES

Very pale skin due to lack of sunlight and larger noses to help us warm cold air

CHANGES

Larger eyes that let in more light to see better in the dark

HOW will ARTIFICIAL LIMBS improve?

The oldest known artificial body parts—also called prostheses—are wooden toes found on mummies from ancient Egypt. For centuries after, artificial limbs were made from wood, metals, or plastic. Now, to make the best prostheses possible, scientists are creating new materials and designs. To do this, they are studying how bodies move—and how the brain works. By studying the tiny bundles of fibers, nerves, and muscles that let people move (see p. 22) and the strength of human bones (see p. 6), scientists are learning to make materials that can bend with human bodies and absorb their weight and movement. They are also developing limbs that can inter-act with the human brain to move as a natural limb would. These are electronic prostheses that will be able to sense messages sent by the wearer's nerve endings and instruct the limb how to move on its own.

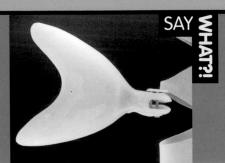

A DOLPHIN THAT LOST HER TAIL IN A FISHING ACCIDENT WAS GIVEN A PROSTHETIC TAIL THAT ALLOWED HER TO SWIM.

SAY WHAT?!

SAY **WHAT?!**

WHAT?!

SCIENTISTS USED A 3D PRINTER TO CREATE A PROSTHETIC BEAK FOR AN EAGLE WHO HAD LOST HERS IN AN ACCIDENT.

In the **FUTURE**, **SCIENTISTS** might be able to grow **REPLACEMENT LIMBS** in a **LABORATORY.**

HOW do ORGAN TRANSPLANTS work?

If the idea of taking an organ from one person and giving it to another seems pretty space age, that's because it is—the first ever organ transplant took place in 1954, just 15 years before the first humans traveled to the moon. An organ transplant is when a healthy organ is given by one person—the donor—to a person with an unhealthy, damaged, or missing organ of the same kind. However, transplants can be very tricky—not only does a donor need to be available, but the donor and the recipient must also be a "match." This means that the organs must be similar in size and their proteins must be similar as well. The reason for this is that a person's immune system—which normally fights off viruses and infections (see p. 11)— might see the new organ as an invader and try to damage it. But with a match, a skilled doctor can encourage the recipient's body to treat the organ as its own.

HUMAN ORGAN

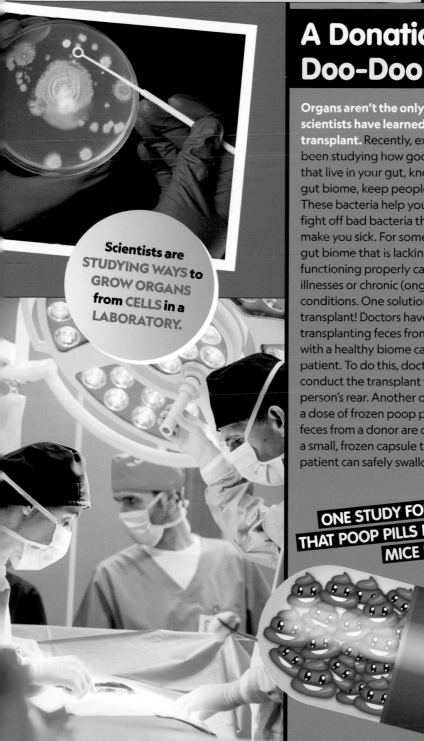

Scientists are STUDYING WAYS to GROW ORGANS from CELLS in a LABORATORY.

A Donation of Doo-Doo

Organs aren't the only thing scientists have learned how to transplant. Recently, experts have been studying how good bacteria that live in your gut, known as your gut biome, keep people healthy. These bacteria help you digest and fight off bad bacteria that could make you sick. For some people, a gut biome that is lacking or not functioning properly can lead to illnesses or chronic (ongoing) conditions. One solution? A poop transplant! Doctors have found that transplanting feces from a person with a healthy biome can help a sick patient. To do this, doctors often conduct the transplant through a person's rear. Another option is a dose of frozen poop pills. The feces from a donor are contained in a small, frozen capsule that the patient can safely swallow.

ONE STUDY FOUND THAT POOP PILLS HELPED MICE LIVE LONGER.

HOW do scientists study NEW DISEASES?

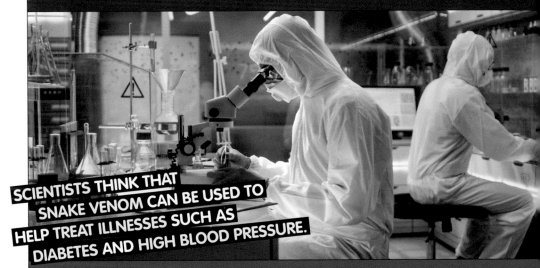

SCIENTISTS THINK THAT SNAKE VENOM CAN BE USED TO HELP TREAT ILLNESSES SUCH AS DIABETES AND HIGH BLOOD PRESSURE.

From the smallest bacteria to the largest animal, organisms are always changing. To keep people healthy and safe, scientists study new diseases whenever they emerge. How do they do this? The first step is safety. Scientists wear special gear—such as gloves, masks, and even protective suits—when working with dangerous diseases. They also work in controlled places such as laboratories. Here, scientists can isolate the disease, or separate it into its own environment. Then scientists watch how the disease infects individual cells. They learn how it spreads and what kind of damage it can cause. This provides the scientists with a lot of information, including who might be at risk from that particular disease, what conditions could cause the disease to spread quickly, where the disease might have come from, and how scientists can fight it.

One ANCIENT EGYPTIAN TEXT recommended putting MOLDY BREAD on CUTS and SCRAPES.

HOW do scientists find NEW CURES?

Once scientists figure out what is causing a disease and how the disease works, they can try to find a cure for it. They often do this by looking for a way to stop whatever the disease is doing "wrong." For example, if a disease has a unique protein that attacks other cells, scientists might find a way to block that protein. Other times, a sick cell might be missing a part, and scientists can try to provide that part.

Finding these answers can take a lot of trial and error—that's why scientists run so many experiments. In fact, one of the keys to a scientist's success is failure! When scientists run an experiment that doesn't work the way they want it to, they can learn a ton about what went wrong. This can help them figure out what might make the experiment go right the next time.

WILL humans be able to LIVE FOREVER?

Humans have long wondered about the ability to live forever—the idea has even inspired spooky tales about immortal vampires and other supernatural creatures. But could scientists make immortality more than just the stuff of fiction? No one really knows. Modern medicine has already created longer life spans for people, and experts see this birthday bonanza improving even more. In fact, some scientists think humans could now live to be 150! Scientists don't know everything about aging, but they do know it has to do with something called telomeres, and that these could be the key to immortality. The ends of a chromosome (see p. 68) are called telomeres. As our cells—and DNA—replicate, telomeres get shorter and shorter, which causes some aspects of aging. If scientists could figure out how to stop telomeres from shortening, perhaps people could live forever.

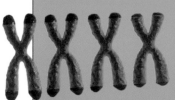

SCIENTISTS THINK THAT GREENLAND SHARKS CAN LIVE UP TO 500 YEARS.

SAY WHAT?!

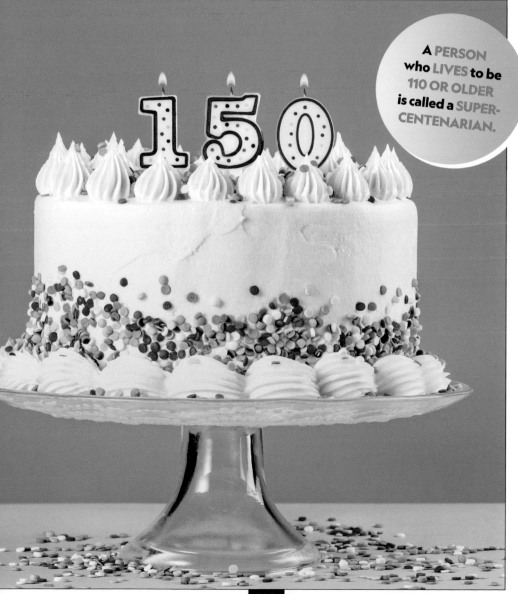

SAY WHAT?!

ONE OF THE OLDEST LIVING ORGANISMS ON EARTH IS A BRISTLECONE PINE TREE CALLED METHUSALEH—IT'S MORE THAN 4,850 YEARS OLD.

A PERSON who LIVES to be 110 OR OLDER is called a SUPER-CENTENARIAN.

CAN a COMPUTER match the HUMAN BRAIN?

In a "human brain vs. computers" intelligence showdown, who's the winner? That depends on whom you ask. Some people say that computers have already outpaced the human brain. After all, computers have beaten people at chess and the Chinese strategy game Go, can solve difficult math problems in the blink of an eye, and never get tired (as long as they have power!). But many scientists say that computers don't yet hold a candle to the complexity of the human brain. For one thing, the brain processes information much more quickly and more efficiently than a computer does. The brain can also adapt to many kinds of external information and stimulation—such as sounds, printed words, touch, and more. Computers can only process the information for which they've been programmed.

SOME POPULAR MUSICIANS HAVE EXPERIMENTED WITH USING ARTIFICIAL INTELLIGENCE TO WRITE NEW SONGS.

Amazing Artificial Intelligence

Artificial intelligence, or AI, is the combination of many different technologies to mimic the way humans learn and solve problems. In many movies, AI refers to synthetic (or artificial) versions of humans that can think and act like we do. Although many experts think that technology may one day progress to that level of intelligence, we're not quite there. In the meantime, AI is probably still very present in your life. Here are some of the cool technologies that rely on AI:

Voice recognition technology: If you've ever used speech to command a phone, you're interacting with AI.

Automatic navigation: Trying not to get lost? AI can help with that!

Autocorrect: Even when it's suggesting a word you don't want, autocorrect is AI.

Face recognition: Whether you're entering a top secret vault or just unlocking an electronic tablet, AI is conducting the face scan.

One scientist claims that in the FUTURE, ARTIFICIAL INTELLIGENCE will be BILLIONS of times SMARTER THAN HUMANS.

WILL robots be able to do SURGERY?

Robots have lots of jobs these days. They work in factories, conduct some trains, vacuum the floors, and even make deliveries. Could robots one day work as doctors? They are already present in the operating room. In addition to the machines that monitor a patient's body and help keep them healthy, many surgeons are using something called robotic-assisted surgery. During these procedures, doctors control robotic cameras and arms that are attached to tiny surgical instruments. This lets the doctor perform surgeries with more control and with fewer incisions, or cuts. However, these robots aren't thinking on their own; the doctors are telling them what to do. But that doesn't mean that self-guided robots aren't a possibility. In fact, scientists are working on developing a worm-shaped robot the size of a thread that could travel into a person's body to fight things that could make them sick.

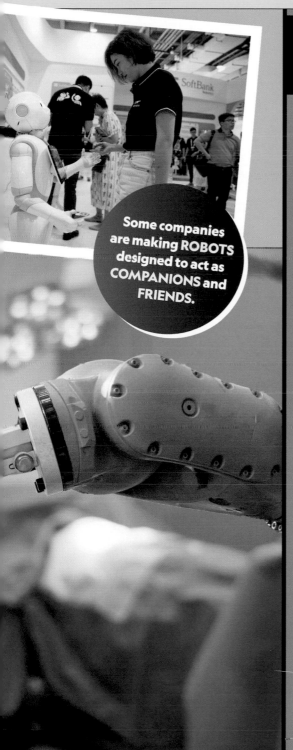

Some companies are making ROBOTS designed to act as COMPANIONS and FRIENDS.

Robots in the Wild

Just as scientists are developing a worm-shaped robot for surgeries, engineers look to animals to inspire many of their robot designs. Try to guess what types of robots these animals inspired!

1. What kind of robot was inspired by a gecko?
a. a fly-catching robot
b. a robot that can climb walls
c. the world's smallest robot

2. A bee was responsible for inspiring which of these robots?
a. a drone about half the size of a paper clip
b. a robot that gives medical shots
c. a robot that plays music

3. A robot inspired by a squid could be used for this purpose:
a. painting walls
b. catching fish
c. moving around on the moon's surface

4. Robots inspired by cockroaches might be used in what kind of situation?
a. search and rescue
b. food testing
c. collecting trash

ANSWERS: 1. b, 2. a, 3. c, 4. a

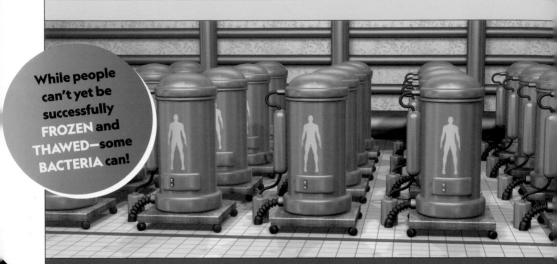

COULD you safely FREEZE yourself?

The idea of being frozen in time only to thaw and come back to life years later might seem weird, but it's one that's been popular since the 1960s. There's even a name for it: cryonics. The concept of being cryogenically frozen, or cryopreserved, involves freezing someone shortly after they die but before their brain activity completely stops. Then, ideally, future technology will be able to unfreeze the person and restore them to life.

Alternatively, writers of science fiction have suggested that brief periods of freezing, known as cryosleep, might act as a sort of pause button for space travelers making long-distance flights. But while scientists have the freezing part down, right now there's no way to reverse the damage that freezing does to a body. Will science ever get there? According to experts, not anytime soon. But it's still great science fiction!

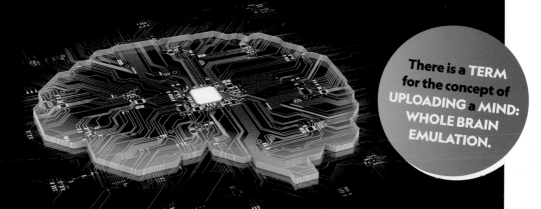

There is a **TERM** for the concept of **UPLOADING a MIND: WHOLE BRAIN EMULATION.**

CAN I UPLOAD my brain?

Immortality might remain out of reach for our human bodies—but according to some experts, it might be a possibility for our brains. Some scientists think that we may one day be able to scan our brains, and then upload that data to a computer. However, experts aren't sure exactly what that means. Computers and brains both learn, store data, and solve problems, but brains are still way more complex than their machine counterparts (see p. 170). Scientists also aren't sure whether the things that makes us *us* would transfer in a scan. Others acknowledge that while the scans might act as a forever storage spot for our memories, they couldn't function as a working brain because they wouldn't be alive. Some scientists think the result could be similar to a virtual avatar, but instead of a character you create, it's a digital version of you that will get to explore a virtual world. No one knows yet if it's possible, but as we understand brains more and more, we're closer to finding out.

WILL I BE ABLE to TELEPORT?

Are we there yet?! Getting from one place to the next can seem to take forever. Wouldn't it be easier to just ... teleport? Unfortunately, teleportation, the ability to transfer something or someone from one point to another without moving through physical space, isn't on the horizons for humans—at least, not anytime soon. This is partly due to the huge amounts of energy teleportation would require. But even more so, it is because of how complex humans are. Every human is made up of tiny building blocks called atoms, which make up living units called cells, which make up organs, and so on. Teleportation would require not only deconstructing all of these materials, but then sending them across space and putting them back together again. Things could get, well, messy! But not to worry—scientists are hard at work thinking of other ways to get from here to there in the blink of an eye.

SOME SCIENTISTS THINK THAT ALTHOUGH WE MAY NOT BE ABLE TO TELEPORT OUR BODIES, WE MAY ONE DAY BE ABLE TO TELEPORT OUR MINDS.

SAY WHAT?!

SAY

WHAT?!

TELEPORTATION **DOES EXIST—** SCIENTISTS HAVE FIGURED OUT HOW TO **TELEPORT** TEENY-TINY PIECES OF MATTER, SUCH AS PARTICLES OF LIGHT.

NOTHING can **MOVE FASTER** than the **SPEED OF LIGHT—**including anything that is **TELEPORTED.**

177

WHY don't CYBORGS EXIST?

Trick question! Cyborgs do exist, and they're likely all around you. You might even be a cyborg yourself! In science fiction, cyborgs are a combination of human and machine that usually has superhuman powers. In real life, cyborgs are human beings that use or rely on bionic parts in their bodies. Today, many prosthetic limbs (see p. 162) are bionic, meaning that they are electronic or mechanical. Other people rely on devices such as pacemakers, which are small robotic devices implanted in a person's chest to help keep their heartbeat regular. As technology improves and scientists get a better understanding of the human body, more and more bionic implants are becoming possible. For example, scientists have developed an implant that can be placed in a person's eye to help restore some eyesight by signaling to the eye's cells the same way light would (see p. 38).

SOME PEOPLE USE BIONIC LEGS THAT WERE INSPIRED BY A CHEETAH'S LEGS AND ARE MEANT FOR RUNNING.

Who's Who of the Future

Cyborg, robot, android—there are lots of futuristic terms to keep track of! Check out this handy chart to tell the difference.

	CYBORG	ROBOT	ANDROID	ARTIFICIAL INTELLIGENCE
IS HUMAN	✓			✓
LOOKS LIKE A HUMAN	✓		✓	
CAN PERFORM PHYSICAL ACTIVITIES AND PROCESSING ON ITS OWN	✓	✓	✓	
CAN "LEARN" AND "THINK" LIKE A HUMAN	✓			✓

WILL my MIND control technology?

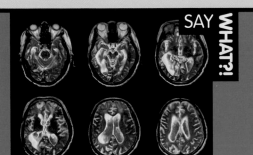

Not all science-fiction technology is impossible to achieve! Scientists are hard at work developing technology that people will be able to control with their minds. In fact, scientists are already creating electric artificial limbs, or bionic limbs, that people can move like natural limbs just by thinking about it (see p. 182). When a person wants to take an action—whether that is taking a step forward, holding a pencil, or making a fist—their brain sends signals to their muscles (see p. 22). These signals tell the muscles to move. Bionic limbs "read" the signals from a person's muscles, then use electricity to interpret the signals as movements— the same way a person's natural limbs would. Scientists are also trying to apply this concept to other technology, such as machines that could scan and interpret a person's brainwaves in order to make a keyboard type using only their mind. It might sound too amazing to be true—but it's real!

SAY WHAT?!

TWO EUROPEAN SCIENTISTS ARE USING SCANS OF HUMAN BRAIN ACTIVITY TO CREATE WORKS OF ART.

SCIENTISTS ARE WORKING ON CREATING TEENY-TINY BIONICS, SUCH AS BIONIC CELLS OR NEURONS.

Some **RESEARCHERS** are developing **ROBOTS** that can be **CONTROLLED** by the **HUMAN MIND.**

BIONICS OF THE FUTURE

Bionics—artificial enhancements or replacements of body parts—have come a long way (see p. 178). How much further will they go? Take a look at some of the bionics that may be developed in the near future.

ELECTRONIC BRAIN IMPLANTS

Some companies are working on the development of brain implants that would allow people to directly interact with computers or other electronics using their minds. This technology would be implanted in a person's brain and then translate their thoughts into actions that control electronic devices.

CONTACT LENS CAMERAS

If you've ever wished you could blink your eyes and capture a moment forever, this one might be for you. Several companies are attempting to create wearable contact lenses that would let people stream images or even videos to nearby devices.

ARTIFICIAL EXOSKELETONS

Scientists have already developed bionic exoskeletons to help improve the mobility of people who were born with mobility issues or have suffered injuries. In the future, developers may take this even further to increase human strength or stamina.

DATA IMPLANTS

If you've ever left home without something you needed, you know forgetting items can be a total pain. Soon, skin implants might cut down on the number of things that can be left at home. Researchers are devising ways to store personal data—such as bank information—in small implants placed below a person's skin. With this data, a person with an implant could potentially pay for an item using just their finger or even unlock an electronic car door.

HEALTH-MONITORING IMPLANTS

Whether in the form of microchip implants, nanobots, or even temporary tattoos, scientists are searching for ways to help alert people to health problems. These tiny forms of bionic technology would be able to monitor a person's various bodily functions—such as heart rate, cholesterol, and more—and then send an alert if an issue is detected.

INDEX

INDEX

INDEX

CREDITS

SS; 95 (all), Gretchen Johnson; **BRAIN:** 96 (UP), Irina Mir/SS; 96 (LO), Africa Studio/AS; 96-97 (UP), BazziBa/AS; 96-97 (LO), Fer Gregory/SS; 97 (1), Redbaron/DR; 97 (2), Luis Louro/AS; 97 (3), martan/SS; 97 (4), Tom Grundy/ASP; 97 (LO), Andrea Izzotti/SS; 98, luismolinero/AS; 99 (UP), Science History Images/ASP; 99 (CTR), Science Photo Library/GI; 99 (LO), Demkat/SS; 100 (LE), Ruth Black/SS; 100-101, Pasieka/Science Source; 101, PIC4U/AS; 102 (LO), Pixelchaos/AS; 102-103 (UP), Cavan Images/AS; 102-103 (LO), Science RF/AS; 103 (UP), Joost van Uffelen/SS; 103 (CTR), Linette Simoes/ASP; 103 (LO), Reinhard Mink/GI; 104 (UP), maximino/SS; 104 (LO), gabriel/AS; 105 (UP), Tory Kallman/SS; 105 (LO), Hero Images/AS; 106 (UP), Pete Saloutos/ASP; 106 (LO), Yefym Turkin/SS; 107 (UP), Yefym Turkin/SS; 107 (LO), khanti jantasao/EyeEm/AS; 108 (UP), Alex Mit/SS; 108 (LO), Buffy1982/AS; 108-109, strmko/GI; 109 (UP), siscosoler/iStock/GI; 110-111, Kwanchai Chai-udom/ASP; 111 (UP LE), Pavel Bobrovskiy/SS; 111 (UP RT), Popova Valeriya/SS; 111 (CTR), Sergey Toropov/AS; 111 (LO), Eric Gevaert/AS; 112 (UP), Kues/SS; 112 (LO), Dan Kosmayer/SS; 113 (UP), Elles Rijsdijk/ASP; 113 (LO), Ezequiel Gim/AS; 114, Fedorov Oleksiy/SS; 115, Tetra Images/ASP; 116 (UP), Jacek Chabraszewski/SS; 116 (LO), Keneva Photography/SS; 117 (UP), Patrick K. Campbell/SS; 117 (LO), Satjawat Boontanataweepol/DR; 118-119 (UP), Sherrod Photography/SS; 118-119 (LO), Renphoto/GI; 119 (UP), Joshua Wanyama/DR; 119 (LO), Andrey Armyagov/SS; 120, Maskot/AS; 121, Lightspring/SS; 122 (UP), Yayayoyo/SS; 122 (LO), Dean Berton-celj/SS; 122-123, Tijana Moraca/SS; 123 (UP), Sabena Jane Blackbird/ASP; 124 (UP), BCFC/SS; 124 (LO), Tatiana Atamaniuk/AS; 125 (both), Rebecca Hale/NGIC; **GROSS:** 126 (LE), clavivs/AS; 126 (RT), Greg Wood/GI; 126-127 (UP), Tatiana Belova/AS; 126-127 (LO), Prostockstudio/DR; 127 (UP), Conner Flecks/ASP; 127 (LO), Joel Sartore/NGIC; 128 (UP), Valentina Razumova/SS; 128 (LO), Lori Epstein/National Geographic Partners; 129 (UP), Carolyn Lagattuta/AS; 129 (CTR), UPI/ASP; 129 (LO), Ethan Daniels/SS; 130 (CTR), Gunita Reine/SS; 130-131 (UP), Jagodka/SS; 130-131 (LO), Wirestock/

AS; 131 (UP), imageBROKER/AS; 131 (CTR), Joel Sartore/NGIC; 131 (LO), Tratong/DR; 132, Bonnin Studio/AS; 133, Kate Chris/SS; 134 (LE), DeingeL_/AS; 134-135, David Tipling/ASP; 135 (UP LE), stanciuc/AS; 135 (UP RT), mgkuijpers/AS; 135 (CTR), Hel080808/DR; 135 (LO LE), Georgi Baird/SS; 135 (LO RT), Dr Morley Read/SS; 136 (UP RT), ThamKC/AS; 136 (LO LE), Naeblys/AS; 137 (UP), bestv/SS; 137 (CTR), soupstock/AS; 137 (LO), Eric Isselée/DR; 138-139 (UP), Irina Markova/SS; 138-139 (LO), Nataliia Prokofyeva/DR; 139 (UP), Ronald Van Der Beek/DR; 139 (CTR LE), Richard Fitzer/SS; 139 (CTR RT), Eric Isselée/SS; 139 (LO), Seregraff/SS; 140 (UP), Ron Greer/SS; 140 (LO), Artur/AS; 140-141, Hero Images/AS; 141 (UP), Oleh Tereshchenko/DR; 142 (UP), Lasse Kristensen/SS; 142 (LO), Will Anderson/AS; 143 (UP), Suprunvitaly/DR; 143 (LO LE), Cynthia Turner; 143 (LO RT), Rob Walls/ASP; 144 (LE), Kraken Images/AS; 144 (RT), Herschel Hoffmeyer/SS; 144-145 (UP), Ryosuke Kuwahara/SS; 144-145 (LO), Natalie Jeffcott/AS; 145 (UP), Konstantin/AS; 145 (LO), Greg Amptman/SS; 146 (UP), Johnfoto/DR; 146 (LO), wildestanimal/GI; 146-147, dundanim/AS; 147 (UP), shootingtheworld/AS; 148 (LE), Cathy Keifer/SS; 148-149 (UP), ShotPrime Studio/AS; 148-149 (LO), Ildar Abul-khanov/GI; 149 (UP), Julia Zavalishina/AS; 149 (LO), Mark Kostich Photog-raphy/AS; 150 (CTR), Mark Dymchen-ko/GI; 150-151 (UP), SciePro/AS; 150-151 (LO), Audrey Shtecinjo/AS; 151 (UP), shchus/AS; 151 (CTR), Dora Zett/SS; 151 (LO RT), Four Oaks/SS; 151 (LO LE), Ann and Steve Toon/ASP;152 (UP), Alexilus/SS; 152 (LO), FurryFritz/AS; 153, Sean Locke Photography/AS; 154 (UP), Yefym Turkin/SS; 154 (CTR), GVS/AS; 154 (LO), Rudmer Zwerver/SS; 154-155, Elnur/AS; 155 (UP), Phonlamai Photo/SS; **FUTURE:** 156 (LE), Halfpoint/AS; 156-157 (UP), Raj Creationzs/SS; 156-157 (LO), DC Studio/AS; 157 (UP), IanDagnall Computing/ASP; 157 (LO), Sashkin/AS; 158 (UP), David Aguilar; 158 (LO), rtype/AS; 159, Terry Virts/NGIC; 160 (UP), sashazerg/AS; 160 (LO), Anna Sedneva/SS; 161 (UP), Stocktrek Images Inc./ASP; 161 (CTR LE), Iakov Kalinin/SS; 161 (CTR), Spirit of America/AS; 161 (CTR RT), Dimitri

Goderdzishvili/SS; 161 (LO LE), schankz/AS; 161 (LO CTR), Gelpi JM/SS; 161 (LO RT), Michael Burrell/ASP; 162 (UP), Jeffrey Isaac Greenberg 10+/ASP; 162 (LO), ZUMA Press Inc/ASP; 162-163, Jose Carlos Cerdeno/AS; 163 (UP), Glen Hush/U.S. Fish & Wildlife Service; 164, nosorogua/AS; 164-165 (UP), Michal Kowalski/SS; 164-165 (LO), gpointstudio/AS; 165 (RT), Viachaslau Kraskouski/SS; 165 (LO) Sanjida Rashid; 166, Gorodenkoff/AS; 167, vchalup/AS; 168 (UP), Science Photo Library/ASP; 168 (LO), Nick Caloyianis/NGIC; 168-169, jfunk/AS; 169 (UP), eye35pix/ASP; 169 (LO), vladvm50/AS; 170 (LO LE), Kirsty Pargeter/AS; 170-171 (UP), metamor-works/SS; 170-171 (LO), Sarah Holm-lund/AS; 171 (LO), Prostock-studio/AS; 172 (UP), kirill_makarov/SS; 172 (LO), romaset/AS; 172-173 (UP), Song fan/AP Photo; 172-173 (LO), Monopoly919/AS; 173 (UP), tanoochai/SS; 173 (CTR), Daniel Prudek/AS; 173 (LO), skydie/SS; 174, Vrx1234/DR; 175 (UP), Lee/AS; 175 (LO), Steve Young/AS; 176 (UP), Valdis Torms/SS; 176 (LO), Jim DeLillo/ASP; 176-177, Leo Lintang/AS; 177 (UP), sergofan2015/AS; 178 (LE), Dreamwood videography - Mikhail Nilov/AS; 178-179, Phonlamai Photo/SS; 179 (UP), sportpoint/SS; 179 (RT), Waxwawax/GI; 180 (UP), Yakobchuk Olena/AS; 180 (LO), MriMan/SS; 180-181, Westend61/AS; 181 (UP), Sebastian Kaulitzki/SS; 182 (LO), dragonstock/AS; 182-183, Sergii Iaremenko/Science Photo Library/GI; 183 (UP), janiecbros/GI; 183 (LO), Alexa Mat/AS

Since 1888, the National Geographic Society has funded more than 14,000 research, conservation, education, and storytelling projects around the world. National Geographic Partners distributes a portion of the funds it receives from your purchase to National Geographic Society to support programs including the conservation of animals and their habitats. To learn more, visit natgeo.com/info.

For more information, visit nationalgeographic.com, call 1-877-873-6846, or write to the following address:

National Geographic Partners, LLC
1145 17th Street NW
Washington, DC 20036-4688 U.S.A.

For librarians and teachers:
nationalgeographic.com/books/librarians-and-educators

More for kids from National Geographic: natgeokids.com

National Geographic Kids magazine inspires children to explore their world with fun yet educational articles on animals, science, nature, and more. Using fresh storytelling and amazing photography, *Nat Geo Kids* shows kids ages 6 to 14 the fascinating truth about the world—and why they should care. **natgeo.com/subscribe**

For rights or permissions inquiries, please contact National Geographic Books Subsidiary Rights: bookrights@natgeo.com

Designed by Amanda Larson

Library of Congress Cataloging-in-Publication Data

Names: Towler, Paige, author.
Title: The human body / Paige Towler.
Description: Washington, D.C.: National Geographic Kids, [2023] | Series: Why? | Includes index. | Audience: Ages 8-12 | Audience: Grades 4-6 |
Identifiers: LCCN 2022003543 | ISBN 9781426374777 (paperback) | ISBN 9781426374784 (library binding)
Subjects: LCSH: Human body--Juvenile literature.
Classification: LCC QP37 .T585 2023 | DDC 612--dc23/eng/20220228
LC record available at https://lccn.loc.gov/2022003543

The publisher would like to thank Paige Towler, author and researcher; Grace Hill Smith, project manager; Avery Naughton, project editor; Lori Epstein, photo manager; Sarah Gardner, associate photo editor; Robin Palmer, fact-checker; Alix Inchausti, senior production editor; and Gus Tello, designer.

Printed in China
23/RRDH/1

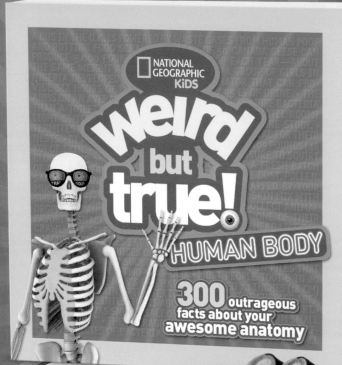